A Simple Guide to John

A Simple Guide to John

Paul J. McCarren, SJ

A SHEED & WARD BOOK

ROWMAN & LITTLEFIELD PUBLISHERS, INC.
Lanham • Boulder • New York • Toronto • Plymouth, UK

A Sheed & Ward Book

Published by Rowman & Littlefield Publishers, Inc.
A wholly owned subsidary of The Rowman & Littlefield Publishing Group, Inc.
4501 Forbes Boulevard, Suite 200, Lanham, Maryland 20706
www.rowman.com

10 Thornbury Road, Plymouth PL6 7PY, United Kingdom

British Library Cataloguing in Publication Information Available

Library of Congress Cataloging-in-Publication Data

McCarren, Paul J., 1943–
A simple guide to John / Paul J. McCarren.
p. cm.
"A Sheed & Ward book."
Includes index.
ISBN 978-1-4422-1878-9 (cloth : alk. paper)—ISBN 978-1-4422-1879-6 (pbk. : alk. paper)—ISBN 978-1-4422-1880-2 (electronic)
1. Bible. N.T. John—Commentaries. I. Title.
BS2615.53.M343 2013
226.5'077—dc23
2012031134

Printed in the United States of America

Contents

Introduction

Why I Needed a Simple Guide to the Gospels

It took me a long time to hear what the Gospels say. Luckily, I spent much of that time with the Jesuits, an organization that is patient with slow learners. Like all the other religious orders in the Catholic Church, the Jesuits attempt to respond to Jesus' command in the Gospels to spread the Good News. So Jesuits are required to take time learning what's proclaimed in the Good News. One method used in this learning process is the Spiritual Exercises of Ignatius Loyola. Most of those exercises are contemplations of Gospel scenes that are undertaken with the help of a director, just as physical exercises are often done with the help of a trainer. Jesuits go through these exercises at least twice. I did the Spiritual Exercises as a Jesuit novice; but when I did them again years later, I was shocked to discover I had no idea what I was doing.

The shock hit me late one afternoon as I read to my director a description of how the exercises had gone that day. As I read, he began to cough and clear his throat. He reached for a tissue and said, "Sorry; please excuse me. I've sometimes cried while listening to a write-up, but I've never laughed so hard." My look must have said, "What's so funny?" So he asked me to listen to what I'd been writing. After he read from notes he'd taken on my write-ups, he said, "Notice how you're picturing Jesus." I'd been imagining Jesus acting as a stern teacher who could barely control his impatience with people's slowness to understand his message. Over and over in my prayers I had seen Jesus as a man who was quick to find fault with the mistakes made by his followers. After asking me to notice that this image wasn't very appealing, my director reminded me that the Gospels describe someone quite different from the Jesus I'd imagined. They tell us, for instance, that many people found Jesus immensely attractive. Some of them even dropped everything to follow him. I had missed this simple fact. How was that possible?

At some point in my life I had slipped into the assumption that, because the Gospels describe a God who is infinite, it must be infinitely difficult to relate to him. The logic of that assumption seemed as obvious as the fact that because the theories of modern physics are extremely complex, physics is extremely difficult to get your mind around. But the Gospels aren't complex theoretical reflections on mysterious truths—and they can't be understood as such. They are four descriptions of how Jesus struggled to share his love of God with others, and how his struggle succeeded. The Gospel writers relate this success to us as simple Good News that Jesus invited others to enjoy and spread.

With the help of my retreat director, I stopped looking for hidden lessons in the Gospel narratives. When I began to reread the Gospels without the prejudice of my assumptions, it became clear that, despite many differences in the four texts, each evangelist's narrative zeroed in on the same thing: Jesus' passionate drive to teach by his words and his actions. Biblical scholars have pointed out that we don't know precisely how the Gospel texts reached the form in which they are now presented in the Bible. The Gospel of Luke glances at this fact when it begins with the note that accounts (yes, he says "accounts") had been handed down to the evangelist's generation by those who had witnessed Jesus' ministry [Lk.1:2]. Then the evangelist promises to organize this material so that the reader might come to "realize the certainty of the teachings" [Lk.1:4]. All the Gospel authors (or, if you like, all the editors and copyists who arranged the work of the original authors into the various manuscripts from which our modern Bibles are translated) seem to share this purpose: to make it plain that Jesus taught about God's determination to bring his work of creation to glorious fulfillment in us, his children.

Years ago on retreat, when my director nudged me to take a careful look at precisely what the Gospels say, I began to see them as attempts to let readers hear what Jesus struggled to teach his first disciples to hear: good news. With my director's encouragement to note the simple facts and details set down by the evangelists, I began to feel that even someone as benighted as myself could begin to take in the Gospel's simple message.

WHY A SIMPLE GUIDE TO THE GOSPELS MIGHT HELP YOU

When I look back on my difficulty in noticing Jesus' simple proclamation of the Good News, I take comfort in the fact that my denseness isn't unique. For example, when Mark describes Jesus visiting Nazareth, his old neighbors are said to be so astonished by his teaching that they couldn't believe it. They ask, "Where did this man get all this?" [Mk.6:2]. What they heard seemed too good to be true, so they resolved the tension they felt between surprise and suspicion by choosing to be annoyed: "They took offense at him" [Mk.6:3]. Mark and the other evangelists relate such moments of rejection as dead ends—moments when the story they're telling comes to a temporary halt. In other scenes, however, doubt and astonishment don't end with a rejection of the Good News but lead to an awareness of its power to move the heart. For example, Luke describes the disciples' first response to seeing Jesus after his resurrection as a mix of bafflement and glee: "They were still incredulous for joy and were amazed" [Lk.24:41]. Here, the disciples' delight is said to be as real as their disbelief. A sense of befuddlement ("How can this be?") grips them even as they're filled with joy. One feeling doesn't cancel the other. Luke is telling us that doubts and suspicions needn't overwhelm us with dismay even when they're striking us with full force. What good news!

If you, like me (and like many disciples before us), have been confused by parts of the Gospel narratives, you too might benefit from some simple comments about each scene and event—such as my director's comment about the people who found Jesus fascinating. And you, like me, might be helped by noting that all of Jesus' followers had to grapple with his simple message before they could accept it. For instance, when the Gospel of Mark describes events after the resurrection, it portrays Jesus taking many disciples to task for their stubbornness: "He appeared to them and rebuked them for their unbelief and hardness of heart because they had not believed those who saw him after he had been raised" [Mk.16:14]. Recall, however, what Jesus says next to these slow learners: "He said to them, 'Go into the whole world and proclaim the Gospel to every creature'" [Mk.16:15]. Here Jesus entrusts the announcement of the Gospel—the Good News—to the very individuals who, when they first heard reports of the resurrection, couldn't believe them. It's natural to assume that, as these first disciples headed off to fulfill their commission to proclaim the Good News, they needed to review with one another what they thought the Good News was. They would have asked one another such questions as, "What was it he said that time we were caught in the storm; and what did we say in response?" As they recalled their various experiences of what Jesus had said and done, they would have helped one another review the recent past until they began to see a clear and communicable message—a message that others could grasp as Good News. In turn, those who heard this message began to write accounts of what they heard so still others could hear about Jesus and his struggle to proclaim God's truth as Good News. Each Gospel proclaims this Good News, but each one proclaims it somewhat differently.

SOME DIFFERENCES YOU CAN EXPECT
TO FIND IN JOHN'S GOSPEL

Literature: the Gospel According to John has literary touches (such as the lyrical opening, or prologue) that tell readers the author wants to wow them. The evangelist—whom we call John although we know no more about him than about the other three evangelists—aims to dazzle us with the truth that God is indeed at work in our lives, drawing us to glory. To stir up a sense of wonder, John depicts Jesus as a teacher who reflects deeply on God's work in us—a teacher who uses vivid images such as light and darkness, shepherds and sheep, zest and thirst, sight and blindness, a vine and its branches, water and blood to express the vibrant power of God's creative work.

Reflections: John's Gospel isn't a history of Jesus' work. Instead, it sets forth scenes in which we see Jesus mulling over the truths he is trying to embody and teach. We read about a Jesus who believes that God speaks to him—is communicating himself to him—and who is therefore intent on taking God in. We hear Jesus struggle to describe this intimate communion to others—and to invite them to share it. Throughout the Gospel, frustration mounts as Jesus' invitation to enter into these reflections is met with skepticism and indignation.

Signs: at the end of Chapter 20, John tells his readers he hasn't written down all that Jesus did. But he hopes the moments he has depicted will lead us to believe that Jesus is the one whom God chose to bring us to fullness of divine life. From the start of John's Gospel, which reminds us that God began creation in order to give himself to us, to its end, where we're invited to trust in Jesus' reassurance that God is still intent on pouring his life into us, this Gospel nudges the reader to ask: Are you open to the signs of God at work in Jesus, or are you blind to them? Do you yearn to live in glorious light, or are you willing to abide in the darkness of death?

For other matters stressed in John's Gospel, see the index.

A TRANSLATION CHALLENGE

The Gospels were written in Greek. Many Gospel translations, including those in lectionaries used for formal church services, have been prepared by commissions of scholars. These translations not only render into English the words of the Greek text but also retain the original rhetorical phrasings. Because ancient Greek phrasing is different from modern English expression, a strictly literal translation is often hard to follow. The simplicity of an evangelist's message can escape us when a translation retains its original (and unfamiliar) turns of phrase.

In the course of a homily, preachers often rephrase the text that's been proclaimed. They want to make sure we know what the text actually says before they comment on it. So, after a reading, they're likely to tell us, "What the evangelist is saying here is . . ." Like a preacher's careful rephrasing of a text, my translation of John's Gospel in this simple guide spells out anything that might be missed or muddled in a strictly literal translation of the original Greek words and phrases. The translation also includes occasional explanatory remarks that, in other translations, are relegated to footnotes or the accompanying commentary. I've put such explanations within the passages to let you keep reading John's Good News without having to stop to look up unfamiliar references.

ACKNOWLEDGMENTS

My comments after each section of my translation are derived from the study of many scripture commentaries. I am indebted in particular to the richness of the notes and commentary by Francis J. Maloney, SDB, published in the Sacra Pagina studies of the New Testament, and to the wealth of information in the notes and commentary of Raymond E. Brown, published as part of the Anchor Bible.

Many people encouraged me during the writing of the manuscript and helped me with comments on it. Thank you to Bridget Leonard, who worked long and hard as a literary agent for this work, and to Carole Sargent for her guidance at Georgetown University's Office of Scholarly and Literary Publication. And thank you to the parishioners at the parishes where I worked—especially to Dorothy Davis, Agnes Williams, Jayne Ikard, and Tom and Mary Biddle. Other helpful comments came from my sister, Morgan, and from my friends Jean Reynolds and Alan Wynroth. I am grateful to my provincial superior of the Maryland Province of the Jesuits, who allowed me time to write this book, and to all my supportive Jesuit companions, especially James P. M. Walsh, SJ.

ONE

Early Days Near the Jordan—the First Followers

THE EVANGELIST'S INTRODUCTION [JN.1:1–18]

[1] *The Word always was.*
   From the very beginning,
   God gave expression to who he is
   by speaking the divine Word—a perfect self-expression.
   How else could it be? What God was, God's Word was.
   [2] *Yes, God's Word was pouring forth in the very beginning.*
   [3] *Whatever came later, came through the divine Word.*
   Nothing springs to life without the divine Word.
   Everything that came about [4] *because of the divine Word*
   was life—divine life. This life—
   this life from the word that God speaks—
   is what enlightens and enlivens us.
   [5] *God's light lights up the dark—*
   a dark we need no longer fear.
   The night cannot resist his light.

<hr>

As he began his Gospel, John may have been thinking of the first words in the Book of Genesis: "In the beginning, God made the heavens and the earth." John, like the author of Genesis, describes God in action—from the beginning, God is expressing himself. According to John, God has always been pouring himself out, giving himself away [vv.1–2]. God's power of giving himself away while still remaining himself will seem impossible to us. True, we'd like to communicate like that—to give others a complete grasp of who we are, what we think, and what we feel. But when we talk, we can only hope that some part of our hearer's heart or brain is connecting with some part of ourselves that we're hoping to reveal. We're grateful for any small sign that we've made ourselves clear—"Oh, to the *right*. Yes, now I see!" We'd like the power to transplant our thoughts and feelings so completely that the hearer feels and understands all we feel and understand. We'd like our self-expression— our word—to be perfect. But it's not. We can only express ourselves partly. But God's self-expression, God's Word, is perfect. When God speaks, God doesn't express ideas; God expresses God. Or, to put it simply, the Word of God is God [v.4].

So, according to the evangelist, God is always pouring himself completely into his Word, and the Word is always fully receiving and revealing who God is. But, he adds, God doesn't want to keep this relationship exclusive. Creation is part of the divine self-expression [v.3]. For those of us who are cynics, this may sound like pious pap. But, right here at the opening of his Gospel, John wants his readers to know that this story of creation—this story of God giving himself away—cannot end badly. This is good news. There's absolutely no question in the author's mind that the dark cloud of human doubt and worry—including the murk of our thoughts and the blindness of our hearts—will be overcome by the divine light [v.5].

This Good News isn't actually new, of course. For example, the evangelist is about to mention that John the Baptist was a witness to the divine light. Although it's conceivable that a first-time Bible reader might hear the Baptist's proclamation as new, any reader who knows stories about the prophets knows that the proclamation is ancient. Most readers would also know that the proclamation has often been ignored—that God has had to repeat his Good News again and again.

⁶ God wanted to make it plain that his intention was to share the divine light. So, God sent into the world a man named John. ⁷ He was sent to tell us about the power and purpose of divine light—to help us believe. [This was the same mission given to the prophets. Like them, John was to tell others the simple truth that God gives himself to us—pours out the divine Word as light and life.] ⁸ John, of course, was not himself the divine light. No; he came into the world to tell us about that light. [Keep in mind what was said above: everything that comes to be in this world comes to be through the divine Word; see v.3.] ⁹ While John was bearing witness to the truth—the truth that the divine light's power permeates the whole world—the divine light was itself entering the world. ¹⁰ As a matter of fact, the Word of God had come into the world. Isn't it odd that we didn't notice the Word? We, whose very existence springs from the divine Word, showed no awareness of him—although he's the one whose very being we share. ¹¹ Astonishing! He came to us as one coming to his home. But his family didn't welcome him.

Note on the evangelist's references to Jews: in discussions of the Gospel According to John, a question eventually arises about whether the evangelist meant to ridicule the Jews for rejecting Jesus. The description in verse 11 of the rejection of God's Word by his own people must certainly refer to the Jews—or, more precisely, to the rejection of Jesus by many Jews. (Although the evangelist hasn't yet mentioned Jesus by name, readers will know that the Word of God is Jesus.) According to all the Gospels, Jesus confined himself primarily to teaching his fellow Jews. So, if anybody was going to dismiss Jesus' teaching, that choice would have to be made above all by his fellow Jews. How, therefore, would it be wrong for the author of this Gospel, or for anyone else, to remark on the irony of this rejection? I'll address other references to "the Jews" as they occur in the text. But for now let's agree that no one can claim to be free from judgment or bias. (Who doesn't enjoy a bit of unflattering gossip; who doesn't feel free to criticize the neighbors?) And yet, for all of us who entertain such judgments, this Gospel has a surprise. It will be sprung in several ways, but perhaps none so directly as a scene added later to the Gospel, where we read about Jesus' encounter with some self-righteous scribes and Pharisees [8:3–11]. Can anyone suppose the author means that it's only the scribes, the Pharisees, or "the Jews" who must reflect on Jesus' words, "Let the one among you who is sinless throw the first stone" [8:7]? We'll see that, when this evangelist refers to "the Jews," he's referring to all of us who find it easy to judge others' faults, but find it difficult to find fault in ourselves.

After noting that the Word was ignored by many who should have welcomed him, the evangelist continues his introduction with a reference to those who received the Word gladly.

¹² *Some people took in the Word. [They believed what the Word revealed about divine life: that we are being enlightened at this moment by divine life; see v.4. And because our life comes from God, we are called children of God. When they believed this,] they saw themselves as God sees us: as God's children.* ¹³ *This relationship isn't something we choose for ourselves. Nor is it an accident of luck or human ancestry. It's not our doing at all. It's an intimate relationship that God is creating with us.*

It's difficult to believe this. John is asserting that God is now struggling, and has always struggled, to forge a bond with us. But the assertion boggles the mind. When the relationship was first mentioned above [v.4], with the words, "This life [of God] is what enlightens and enlivens us," the statement's abstract quality may have struck the reader with no more force than a song lyric—"You light up my life!" But here [vv.12–13], we have a declaration that is as fantastical as the ending of a fairy tale: "And the foundling was revealed to be the son of the king!" Can such a thing be true of us? Are we the children of a divine creator-king?

We know that ordinary citizens who answer their phone and hear someone announce, "The president is on the line for you," usually report that their first reaction was to protest, "The president! For me? That's impossible!" Why, we wonder, would the president call me? The same is true when God reaches out to us. Perhaps the most famous example of this instinctive disbelief is Mary's response to the Lord's messenger as it's described in the Gospel According to Luke. When the angel tells Mary, "The Lord is with you," she wonders what such a greeting might mean [Lk.1:28–29]. Of course it means exactly what it says: "The Lord is with you!" Like the rest of us, Mary found it hard to believe this. However, unlike many of us, Mary chose to believe it. Although she's never mentioned by name in the Gospel According to John, she must be numbered among those whom the evangelist describes as people who "believed what the Word revealed" [v.12].

John concludes his description of God constantly pouring himself out by reminding us how the Word came to us.

¹⁴ *The Word made a home with us. Yes, the Word took life in the same abode that we have—the body. What we were seeing when we saw the embodied Word was the glory of God made present to us—God's own glory, in the flesh!* ¹⁵ *We have a witness to this truth in John the Baptist. John didn't gaze at the appearance of the eternal Word in silent stupefaction. As we're about to see, he cried, "Look! I've been telling you about this man. I told you, 'There is someone coming to whom you must listen more faithfully than to me because, unlike me, he's always speaking to you [pouring out the divine self]—from the beginning!'"* ¹⁶ *John the Baptist's words are addressed to all of us. We're all receiving the full outpouring of the divine Word—and we're always receiving it. To make this truth apparent, we're now given the Word of God to replace the old gift of the word of the Law.* ¹⁷ *Once, the gift of the Law was presented to us through the mediation of Moses. Now, God's gift of himself is given to us directly in Jesus.*

[18] *Because no one actually sees the God who is reaching out to us, we need a go-between, someone who truly understands the divine relationship that God wants with us. So, God's Word [God's Son, the one who is most intimately God's self-expression,] became one of us in order to make their intimate relationship visible.*

—⁂—

Despite the plainness of the truth laid out in this brief introduction, most readers probably know the truth won't be accepted by many people who appear in the story that follows. In fact, confusion and tension fill the very first scene. The Gospel's introduction tells us that John the Baptist was an eager witness to the truth. But, as we're about to see, his testimony was hotly challenged.

JOHN THE BAPTIST IS CHALLENGED BY THE JERUSALEM AUTHORITIES [JN.1:19–28]

[19] *Priests and Levites went out to John from Jerusalem asking who he thought he was. [20] Coming straight to the point, John said, "Perhaps you think I'm posing as the Messiah—God's Anointed One. I am not the Messiah." [21] "Then who do you claim to be?" they asked. Are you Elijah [who is supposed to return 'before the day of the Lord'; Mal.3:23]?" John gave them a definite "No." So they asked, "Are you claiming to be the Prophet [the one promised to Moses long ago; Dt.18:15]?" Again he said, "No." [22] So, they asked again, "Who are you? We have a commission from Jerusalem to question you. Speak up. Explain yourself." [23] John said, "Remember the words of the prophet Isaiah, 'Look for the Lord even in the wilderness' [Is.40:3]. I'm saying the same thing. Listen to the voice of God. It's crying out to you from everywhere. Don't put up road blocks. Smooth a path for it." [24] Some Pharisees were in this delegation from Jerusalem. [25] They kept pushing for an answer: "If you don't claim to be the Messiah, or Elijah, or the Prophet, why are you baptizing?" [26] John told them he was using water in a ritual of repentance—of turning to God. And then he said, "There's someone right here in your midst who can truly bring you into the presence of God. But you don't notice him. [27] He'll come to your attention nonetheless. I'll give you a hint about his greatness. I can't presume to unstrap his sandal for him." [28] This encounter*

with John happened at the Jordan, where he was preaching and baptizing. It was near Bethany.

———— ⚬⚬⚬ ————

The evangelist begins this first scene of the Gospel with voices of protest. It's like opening a movie with a shot of a car being pulled over by a cop, followed by a shot of the cop asking the driver, "Didn't you see the stop sign back there?" The viewer supposes that the driver has apparently broken an obvious law. In John's Gospel, Jewish authorities, like the film cop, are certain that a rule has been broken — that John the Baptist was teaching without proper author-ization. Notice that the Baptist doesn't contradict their opinion about Jewish teaching and tradition. But neither does he let their unfriendly and disruptive questions alter his witness. There's no need for their special investigation into his intentions. The Baptist has no hidden motive. All he has to say, he is saying openly. And he will keep repeating his witness — even to official investigators from Jerusalem. For John the Baptist, life is a simple matter of giving witness to the basic truth that the divine Word will be made known.

This first scene of the Gospel depicts the boldness of the Baptist's witness as well as the tension it caused. The next scene finds John continuing to give the same witness. But it contains a difference.

JOHN THE BAPTIST RECOGNIZES JESUS AS "THE LAMB OF GOD" [JN.1:29–34]

29 The next day, the Baptist sees Jesus walking toward him and he says, "Look, here is the Lamb of God." [Yes, he was saying that this was God's perfect servant who, like a lamb, follows the Lord's commands.] "He takes away the sins of the world." [Yes, he was saying that the Lamb can turn others away from sin, leading them instead toward God. If they let the Lamb lead them, they, like the Lamb, will serve only God; they will no longer sin by turning away from him.] 30 "This is the one — the one I told you about when I said, 'There's someone coming who is much greater than me. You must listen to him because he speaks to you always — from all eternity' [see v.15]. 31 I don't know him [i.e., I can't pretend to know what he knows about perfect repentance]. I'm cleansing you with water because I want you to get to know him."

As John describes him, the Baptist seems worried that his listeners might not accept his straightforward introduction of Jesus as the "Lamb of God." We can imagine him sensing in them a reluctance to turn their attention from him, whom they'd come to know through his preaching and baptizing, to this stranger. It would be natural for the crowd to feel a certain leeriness—the same leeriness anyone might feel when someone makes an extraordinary claim about something, and then suddenly says, "Here, see for yourself. Go ahead. Look!" Should we look? Do we want to get involved in something we're not sure of? So, says John, the Baptist gave his listeners something other than their suspicions to think about.

[32] "Pay attention to me," John said. "I saw the Spirit. Yes, I saw the divine Spirit, the Spirit of God, stoop to him like a dove [like a dove returning to its dovecote like a bolt from the blue]. The Spirit rushed upon him as though going home. And there it settled and stayed. [33] Trust me when I say that this is not my personal opinion or judgment. Quite the opposite. The same God who inspires me to baptize you with water also inspires me to say: Notice how the Spirit of divine glory clings to this man! Let God press this same glorious Spirit upon you. Let yourselves be awash in the divine Spirit. [34] Parents hope that their spirits will somehow touch their children. But the Spirit of God rushes right into this child, Jesus—Jesus, the Son of God."

According to John, the Baptist has been telling people that someone is coming—someone who not only knows God's promise of love but also accepts and embodies that love unconditionally. That someone is now here. It's time for the Baptist to exit—which he does in the next scene.

JESUS ATTRACTS DISCIPLES [JN.1:35–42]

³⁵ The day after he said all this about Jesus, John the Baptist was again down by the river. Two of his disciples were with him. ³⁶ Jesus was walking in the area. And again John said, "Look, the Lamb of God." ³⁷ John's two disciples heard this and followed Jesus. ³⁸ When Jesus saw they were following him, he asked, "What are you looking for?" Although they were John's disciples, they addressed him as "Teacher," and they asked, "Where are you staying?"

As John presents their question, it might simply mean they wanted to know whether or not Jesus had established a home base as a rabbi and teacher. But we might also imagine they felt like modern applicants to college who, anxious about their choice of school, want to find out more about the curriculum before putting down a deposit. These potential transfer students from John needed a tour, and Jesus invited them on one.

³⁹ Jesus said, "Come see for yourselves." So, off they went to see where he was staying. They didn't go anywhere else that day. ⁴⁰ Andrew, one of the two disciples who'd followed Jesus after hearing John call him the Lamb of God, had a brother named Simon "Peter." ⁴¹ The first thing Andrew did after spending time with Jesus was to find "Peter" and tell him, "We've found out who the Messiah is!" ⁴² So he brought him to where Jesus was staying. Jesus simply looked at Simon "Peter" and said, "You're known as Simon—just as your father is known as John. You will be known as Peter" [i.e., "Rocky," or "the Stonelike One"].

A reader might wonder what Andrew and Simon talked about as they went to meet Jesus. Did Andrew tell him that his teacher, the Baptist, had proclaimed Jesus the Lamb of God? Did Andrew say John's proclamation had inspired him and another disciple to follow Jesus? How did he explain his certainty that Jesus was the

Messiah? In sum, what exactly did they expect to find in Jesus? They may have been hoping to find a person who matched their idea of what a teacher, leader, and messiah should be—that is, their interest in Jesus might not have been different from the interest the Jewish authorities had in John the Baptist. True, the authorities seemed suspicious, whereas Andrew and Simon seem interested. But the authorities wanted to confirm their suspicions by deciding for themselves what the Baptist was attempting to achieve (see vv.19–22). Similarly, Andrew's boast to have identified the Messiah, and Simon's nickname, "Rocky," suggest strong personalities who are likely to hold strong opinions. Will Andrew's cockiness and Simon's toughness make them ready pupils for Jesus' teaching? Aside from a few hints, John leaves us to find out for ourselves what kind of disciples these two will become.

JESUS TRIES TO RAISE HIS DISCIPLES' EXPECTATIONS
[JN.1:43–51]

⁴³ The next day, Jesus, after deciding he wanted to travel to Galilee, noticed Philip and said, "Come with us." ⁴⁴ Philip was from the same town as Peter and Andrew—Bethsaida. ⁴⁵ Then Philip tracked down Nathanael and told him, "We've discovered the Prophet promised to Moses [Dt.18:15; see v.21 above]. His name is Jesus, son of Joseph. He's from Nazareth." ⁴⁶ "From Nazareth!" said Nathanael. "What good do you expect from that place?" Philip said, "Come and see." ⁴⁷ Next, Jesus saw Nathanael walking toward him, and he said, "Here's a real Israelite. But there's no guile in him." [Remember, "Israel" was the name given to Jacob, who was considered a sly character for cheating his brother, Esau, for the firstborn's blessing from their father, Isaac; Gn.27.] ⁴⁸ Nathanael said, "How do you know about me?" Jesus told him, "I saw you under the fig tree before Philip called out to you." ⁴⁹ Nathanael said, "O, teacher, you must be the Son of God—the King of Israel!" ⁵⁰ "Oh?" said Jesus. "You're a believer because I said I saw you under the fig tree? Wait. You'll see more than that. ⁵¹ O, yes; O, yes. O yes, indeed, I say you'll see the sky open up. You'll see God's messengers coming down from heaven and returning there on behalf of the Son of Man."

Events move quickly in this sequence as John depicts Philip's enthusiasm and Nathanael's cockiness in reaction to Jesus. Although John describes Jesus' invitation to Philip as almost casual [v.43], he portrays Philip's reaction as the kind of excitement that follows a great discovery and is expressed by boasting [v.45]—excitement which John shows us Nathanael instinctively deflating [v.46a]. But we see Philip undeterred and throwing back a challenge [v.46b]. Instantly, the scene changes, and we hear Jesus joking about Nathanael's famous ancestor, Jacob—or Israel—and claiming that, unlike his cagey kin, Nathanael is without guile [v.47]. This, and the exchange that follows it, sounds like a snatch of dialogue overheard on the street: "Me?" "Yes, you." "You're kidding me!" [vv.48–49]. What are they talking about? We obviously don't know how Jesus learned about Nathanael from a sighting under a fig tree, or precisely why that knowledge made such an impression on Nathanael, because John doesn't explain any of that. But what John does make clear is that Nathanael, like Philip (see v.45) and Andrew (see above, v.41), thought he knew what to expect from God's chosen one. Then John suddenly describes Jesus bringing this blurry rush of encounters and expectations into focus. First, he challenges Nathanael's notion about what's impressive [v.50]. Then he tells them all—including Andrew, Simon, and Philip—what their expectations for a Messiah should be: they should expect to see the angels of God working diligently "on behalf of the Son of Man" [v.51]. One wonders what they made of that promise—and of that title.

For those of us who think of God as distant, mysterious, and grand, Jesus' choice of the title "Son of Man" may seem odd. If Jesus wanted to associate himself in people's minds with a God of bedazzling power, why not choose "Son of Light," or "Son of Power," or some such lofty title? On the other hand, what nickname would be a better reminder of what the scriptures say God wants to do with his power? For the scriptures tell us God expressed his power by creating human beings in his own image [Gn.1:27]—as his children. If you were a child of angels, that would be something quite special.

But what an astonishingly exalted place you hold because you're a human child—a son of man. To contemporary ears, the title may have an unfortunate sound of male exclusivity. But for the authors of such works as the Book of Daniel and the Book of the Prophet Ezekiel, the title was their way of proclaiming their belief that, one day, someone human-born would fully accept God's gift of "sonship" and would live as a perfect child of God. Here, John describes Jesus telling his first followers that they should not only share this belief but should also expect to see it revealed in him. The next chapter tells us how Jesus' actions began to help his followers glimpse the truth of this astonishingly intimate relationship between God and human beings.

TWO

Jesus at a Wedding in Galilee; Jesus Visiting Jerusalem

GOD'S GLORY IS REVEALED IN JESUS' RESPONSE
TO A NEED AT CANA [JN.2:1–12]

¹ Three days later, there was a wedding in the town of Cana, in Galilee. Jesus' mother was there. ² Jesus too was invited, along with the disciples that had begun to follow him. ³ The wine ran out in the middle of the celebration, so Jesus' mother told him, "There's no more wine." ⁴ Jesus said, "Ma'am, how does this concern of yours involve me? This isn't my hour. This isn't the moment to accomplish my work." [See what was said above: "The Word came home to us. What we saw in the Word was the glory of God"; 1:14. Jesus' "work" is to reveal that God's glory is already present in us. He doesn't think it's yet time for that revelation.] ⁵ His mother told the waiters, "Do whatever he tells you."

————◦◦◦◦————

If we hadn't already noticed, this scene makes it clear that the evangelist supposes his readers are familiar with the Jewish context of Jesus' life. In order to follow the Gospel narrative, we should know about the Patriarchs, Abraham, Isaac, and Jacob; about the message of the prophets; about God's intention to keep sending prophets to his people; and about his people's hope for a special prophet—an

Anointed One, a Messiah. Readers should also be aware that teachers such as John the Baptist and Jesus attracted disciples when, like prophets before them, they interpreted the scriptures and proclaimed God's faithfulness to his Covenant. The evangelist also presumes, as he unfolds the wedding scene, that readers should know that a Jewish wedding feast of the time involved many guests, many days, and plenty to eat and drink. John presumes as well that the reader knows something about Jesus' mother—especially her reputation for trust. With that in mind, let's review the brief but complex encounter that opens the scene at Cana.

First of all, even if readers didn't know a Jewish wedding feast was usually stocked with plenty to eat and drink, they would nonetheless sympathize with people who failed to provide enough wine for their wedding guests [v.3]. Second, when John describes Mary in this scene not by name but as the "mother of Jesus," readers can be forgiven for thinking he wants to evoke the unique influence of mothers on their children. Third, any reader is bound to be surprised by Jesus' response to his mother's mention of the embarrassing lack of wine [v.4a]. Fourth, readers who know something about Mary's famous trust in God may wonder why Jesus doesn't respond to her comment as an expression of faith and trust. Fifth, the curt way in which Jesus refers to his hour [v.4b] gives the impression he thinks his mother should know he's waiting for a particular moment to accomplish a specific task. And a reader might also ask: did Mary know Jesus was waiting to accomplish one specific divine work—and, if so, why did she ask him to do this one too? Finally, if Jesus' response to Mary is meant to remind her that he intends to do only the one task that has been assigned to him, a reader might wonder why Mary nonetheless tells the waiters to expect some direction from Jesus [v.5].

Tension is everywhere in this scene: we can presume the host is embarrassed; the wait staff will be anxious about how to proceed; Jesus seems upset by his mother's comment; and the reader may be edgy about the standoff between mother and son. Mary alone seems unperturbed—trusting. At this point, we might recall what John told us in his introduction: "We need not fear the dark. God's light lights up the night" [1:5]. If we need fear nothing, if God's light can shine anywhere, then the divine light can shine through the anxiety that looms over this wedding. When Jesus' mother tells the waiters, "Do whatever he tells you," her trust may remind Jesus that God's power can break through anywhere.

———◦◯◦———

⁶ At the house where the wedding celebration was taking place, there were six stone water jars. The water was necessary for the many Jewish rituals of washing and purification. Each jar could hold between twenty and thirty gallons of water. ⁷ Jesus told the waiters to make sure each jar was full. So they topped them off. ⁸ When they'd finished, Jesus said, "Take some, and give it to your manager." And they did so. ⁹ Of course the waiters thought they knew they were taking water to the manager. But when he tasted it, it was wine. Not knowing the true source of the wine, the manager approached the bridegroom. ¹⁰ He said, "People usually serve good wine first. Then, after the guests have finished that, they serve something inferior. But you've chosen to serve the good wine now!" ¹¹ This was the beginning of Jesus' signs. At Cana in Galilee he first revealed God's divine glory. It was when his disciples began to understand what it might mean to believe in him. ¹² When the wedding feast was over, Jesus left Cana. With his mother, brothers, and disciples he traveled to the town of Capernaum. But their stay there was short.

———◦◯◦———

The climax of this scene may look like a conjurer's trick. All tension in the scene seems to disappear magically after Mary inspires Jesus to act. However, after delighting in Jesus' power to produce wine from water, readers might be troubled by a question. How exactly was his compassionate response to the need of this couple a revelation of God's glory? In fact, we can suppose that was the question Jesus was putting to his mother when he asked her what connection she thought there might be between him and the wedding couple's pressing need. Notice that John doesn't describe her making a personal appeal to her maternal status. Instead, her words to the wait-

ers simply indicate that she trusts Jesus knows what to do. John
doesn't say what Mary's trust was based on; but he's already told us
Jesus was interested in doing only what the Father wants. (All *our*
desires, on the other hand, are clouded with self-interest.) So,
Mary's apparent trust that Jesus will do God's work at this moment—that he will not be acting merely out of the goodness of his
own heart—seems to free him to do God's work, not his own. As
John has described it, Mary's behavior is testimony to her trust that
God is at work in all our needs. And Jesus affirmed her witness. It's
a witness central to John's understanding of the Good News. In the
introduction he said, "Whatever came later, came through the divine Word—nothing springing to life without it" [1:3]. If God's gift
of himself to creation fills the world with divine glory, how
wouldn't all the moments of this couple's life—good moments and
bad—be bursting with the divine presence?

The Word of God, of course, knows this. But Jesus, like us, is also
human. Like us, he learns. As John's Gospel unfolds and Jesus continues to travel and teach, we'll see Jesus learn more and more
about the work of God's presence. Some people will accept his
unique experience of God's presence. Others will ignore or misunderstand it—for instance, in the next scene. The scene is also
another example of the author's assumption that readers know
something about Jewish religious customs. In this case, it's the an-
nual Jewish celebration of God's "passing over" his people—the
time when God enveloped them in safety and fulfilled his promise
to free them from Egyptian captivity.

DURING PASSOVER IN JERUSALEM, JESUS CHALLENGES
MERCHANTS IN THE TEMPLE [JN.2:13–25]

*[13] Because the Jewish feast of Passover was approaching, Jesus traveled to
Jerusalem to celebrate it. [14] He entered the Temple court and found there men
selling livestock and poultry [to people who hadn't brought sacrificial animals
with them]. Also there, for people's convenience, were booths with money men
[ready to make the correct change for paying the Temple tax or buying sacrificial*

offerings]. [15] *Jesus made a flail out of some ropes, and chased all those men from the area, stampeding the livestock and spilling the money as well.* [16] *He ordered the men with the dove boxes, "Take the birds with you." He called out to them all, "Stop making my Father's house a bazaar."* [17] *His disciples saw this and thought of the Psalm verse, "My only obsession is the house of the Lord" [Ps.69:9].* [18] *The Jewish authorities saw it and said, "What sign gives you the right to do this?"* [19] *Jesus said, "[Let this be a sign for you.] Go ahead and ruin the Temple. I'll create another in three days."* [20] *Their response was: "What took forty-six years to build, you're going to replace in three days?"* [21] *They didn't imagine he was talking of something besides the Temple building—that he was speaking of himself.* [22] *His disciples, on the other hand, recalled these words after Jesus was raised from the dead. Then they realized that scripture's descriptions of faith, dedication, zeal, and righteousness matched Jesus' actions. It was also then, at last, that they truly believed what Jesus had taught them.* [23] *During this Passover visit of Jesus to Jerusalem, many put faith in his name. They liked the signs they saw.* [24] *However, Jesus wasn't taken in by this show of belief. He understood them well.* [25] *He didn't need lessons in human behavior. He already understood it.*

———❦———

The outrage Jesus instinctively expresses for the abuse of the Temple might seem a bit extreme to anyone who chooses to go along to get along. Why make a fuss? Isn't it sensible to sell animals for sacrifice? Why should pilgrims have to bring animals from homes far from Jerusalem? And surely it would be a relief for pilgrims to manage potentially confusing money transactions through professional banking types conveniently located in the Temple.

But Jesus seems to be offended that people should let Temple "business" distract them from the Temple's only purpose. Jesus' passionate display comes down to a simple question for all who are in the Temple: What are you here for? The reader of this Gospel knows that the only person who can answer that question clearly is Jesus because Jesus, as we saw above, is the divine light that is breaking through the darkness [1:5].

John tells us Jesus seems to have impressed some people in Jerusalem because of signs they saw [v.23]. But John quickly adds that Jesus didn't trust their show of faith in signs [vv.24–25]. This gloomy assessment of Jesus' reaction to apparent believers may puzzle a reader who forgets the context of Jesus' words and actions: Jesus is living with and speaking to the people of God. And if they're truly God's people, why would they look for signs to tell them what they already know? True, it may seem sensible for the people of God to look for signs to help them remember their special relationship with God. After all, it's natural for anyone who puts their faith in someone to look for a sign that their trust isn't misplaced. ("Trust, but verify," we tell ourselves.) Ask yourself if you'd like to experience some of the signs received by the people of God in the past. For instance, do you admire Moses' miraculous signs—especially his ability to get people out of life-threatening situations? Do you think it would be easier to have faith if you heard a prophet speak with miraculous powers of persuasion? Would you believe more deeply in God if you could experience just a little more . . . what? What signs do you need in order to believe? What signs do you imagine the Passover crowds heard and saw Jesus accomplish that led them to say they believed in him? The simple answer to the question of what signs are needed in order to believe is that there can be no sign that leads directly to belief. If someone makes you a promise, you can't know for sure the promise is true until it's actually fulfilled. In the case of the people of God, to whom John describes Jesus speaking, they can choose to doubt God's ability to fulfill his promise to care for them, or they can choose to trust his promise. Up to now, the people whom Jesus has encountered in Jerusalem have seemed filled with worry and doubt. Jesus is about to meet another such person.

THREE

Nicodemus Is Baffled; the Baptist's Disciples Are Baffled

IN JERUSALEM, JESUS POINTS OUT NICODEMUS'S LACK OF FAITH [JN.3:1–15]

[1] *[Jesus had been in Jerusalem during Passover.] In Jerusalem was a man named Nicodemus who, as a Pharisee, was a member of the ruling body of the Jews.* [2] *Nicodemus visited Jesus one night. Calling him "Teacher," he told him, "We realize your teaching is from God. You can't produce the signs you've produced unless God is with you."* [3] *"O, yes; O, yes. O yes, indeed," said Jesus, "I too realize that no one sees or experiences God's presence unless they're born from it."* [4] *"Born?" said Nicodemus. "Born a second time? How's that possible? Once you're out of the womb, you can't go back—especially if you're full-grown!"* [5] *"O, yes; O, yes. O yes, indeed, I mean just what I say," said Jesus. "It's impossible for you to enter or experience the presence of God unless that's where you're from in the first place—I mean, unless you are born from it by water and the Spirit."*

—⊙⁄⊙⟞

Though Nicodemus speaks of signs and addresses Jesus as "Teacher," John describes Jesus focusing on Nicodemus's claim that "God is with you" [v.2] and suggesting that Nicodemus didn't know

19

what that meant (cf. 1:12–13). Then John describes Nicodemus as indeed puzzled by Jesus' description of experiencing God's presence [vv.3–4]. From the start of this Gospel, John has emphasized God's struggle to give himself to us—to be with us. Here, John portrays Nicodemus as certain that no one gets a second chance at life. John then reports Jesus' invitation to imagine the possibility of being born in, or coming alive to, God's Spirit [v.5].

⁶ "Look; what's born of flesh? Flesh! But what's born of Spirit is Spirit. ⁷ You can't possibly be surprised I said that everyone must be born from the divine Spirit! [Are you so distracted by your body's needs and limitations that you think the Spirit can't permeate you—can't bring God alive in you?] ⁸ Listen a moment to the wind. Hear it blow wherever it wants. You can't predict its moves. Do you think you can understand the Spirit's moves?" ⁹ Nicodemus nonetheless asked, "How exactly does this work? How do you achieve birth from Spirit?" ¹⁰ But Jesus answered, "You're a teacher of your fellow Jews, and you don't already know the answer to this question? ¹¹ O, yes; O, yes. O yes, indeed, I speak of what I'm certain [when I speak about being born from above—from God]. ¹² If you don't believe the things already revealed here on earth [i.e., what the scriptures say about our relationship with God], how will you believe me if I reveal our heavenly relationship with God? ¹³ Nobody has gone up to heaven—except, of course, the one who has come down from heaven. I mean the Son of Man. ¹⁴ Remember how Moses raised up the serpent in the wilderness? That's how the Son of Man must be raised up. ¹⁵ Yes, raised up so that people might believe, and have eternal life."

One wonders at this point if Nicodemus was sorry he came to visit. According to John, after flattering Jesus with the title "Teacher," Nicodemus found himself not only being taught [vv.6–8] but also having his own aptness for teaching being questioned [vv.9–10]. This questioning isn't impolite, however. It's an attempt to help Nicodemus confront the fact that everyone's instinctive response to

God's promise is disbelief. Jesus nudges Nicodemus to notice that his trust in God's promise—a promise offered again and again in the scriptures—must be a little weak if he can't imagine that God is capable of bringing him to birth in the divine Spirit [vv.13–15].

Did Jesus' mention of going to and coming from heaven [v.13] make things more clear for Nicodemus, or less? We can't answer that question because Nicodemus isn't heard from again in this scene. But the question is actually for us. What do *you* make of Jesus' comments? We can't know whether Jesus' words referring to himself as "one who has come down from heaven" [v.13] are intended by the evangelist to suggest that Jesus had an awareness of being the embodied Word of God. But there is an obvious way in which the human Jesus—the Son of Man—has already gone to heaven, though he hasn't yet died. He's gone to heaven inasmuch as his desire, hope, and very being are turned over to the Father in heaven. Jesus has accepted completely the truth that his life is not his, but belongs to his heavenly Father. He is totally, blissfully united with him. Or to put it another way, he has gone up to heaven.

Jesus' way of asserting that he must be lifted up [v.14] would be recognizable to Nicodemus, an educated Jewish leader, as a reference to an episode during the journey of the people of God through the wilderness (Num.21:4–9). The episode describes how the people panicked when they encountered poisonous snakes on their journey—even though they had already received many signs that God knew, and cared for, their needs. Then God is described offering another sign: Moses was to raise up a bronze figure of a serpent. If the people looked upon that figure, they would be healed of their bites—that is, the bronze sculpture should remind them who cures all their ills. Jesus is telling Nicodemus that the Son of Man is to be raised up for a similar purpose—to bring God's healing and life to believers.

If readers understand Jesus' statement as a reference to his crucifixion, they might wonder, as a practical matter, how raising Jesus on a cross brings eternal life. Readers might also ask whether they're supposed to imagine that Jesus' words to Nicodemus are historically accurate. Does the evangelist think that Jesus knew and spoke about the manner of his death from the beginning of his days of teaching? The question of historical accuracy, and the theological question of how, precisely, Jesus' dying gives divine life, are interesting distractions, but they are distractions nonetheless. Although John might have hoped to provoke reflection on such matters, it's not likely he would have wanted his readers to miss his main point. His main point here seems to be that Jesus was leading Nicodemus to ask a question when he told him the Son of Man would be raised up in order to bring eternal life to all. It's the same question John has already posed in various ways. It comes down to this: if you truly believe that God's light is coming into the world, do you think anything can block or overcome that light? Or to put it another way: because you can't figure out how God will manage to bring his divine plans for you to a perfect, joyous conclusion, do you suppose that God is also puzzled by his plans? Are you worried that something might prevent God from fulfilling his plan?

John seems to assume that everyone has trouble believing. He therefore offers some comments for reflection.

THE EVANGELIST COMMENTS ON JESUS' DESIRE TO GIVE US DIVINE LIGHT [JN.3:16–21]

[16] *Imagine how much God loves this world. He's giving his only Son—the Word, the complete expression of himself—to all of us. He wants to show us how to embrace eternal life, not death.* [17] *God didn't send the Son to condemn us for our doubts and selfish inclinations, but to save us from them.* [18] *It should be obvious that, if you let the Son save you from selfish choices, you won't be condemned for them. It's also obvious that those who reject God's saving power are already condemned. They condemn themselves by clinging to their narrow notions and by refusing to believe that God cares enough to send his Son to help them.* [19] *Do you see why some are condemned? Divine light is pouring down on them, but they seek the dark. People choose the dark when they're addicted to their evil deeds and can't imagine anything but their addiction.*

[20] *Those who do evil [i.e., those driven only by what they want] don't like light on their work. If they go near the light, their selfishness will be exposed for what*

it is. ²¹ If you seek to do what's right, what's true, you'll need God's light. And when you seek God's light, you'll find it already at work in you! Those who notice that you're seeking will see you searching for God's light .

The evangelist's description of Jesus' conversation with Nicodemus, and his comments here, constitute a lesson that has unfolded in a series of simple questions leading directly to an obvious conclusion: Do you see this? Yes? Now, do you see that? Yes? Now, do you see that this and that are connected? Yes? Then, there you have it!

Because Jesus is a teacher, those who want to be his students must be willing to learn—must be able to admit their ignorance. Willing students are usually delighted to find a tutor who teaches with simplicity—a tutor like this evangelist. In his comments above, John describes what Jesus wants to teach (to Nicodemus, to the pilgrims in Jerusalem, to his disciples, and to anyone who will listen to him). His description is quite simple and can be summarized this way: human understanding of divine life is incomplete [vv.16–17], but Jesus understands divine life completely. If we let him fill our lives with divine light, we too will grasp God's life fully [v.18]. If we reject God's light, we're condemned to remain in our ignorance [v.19]. We can choose either the light of understanding or the darkness of disbelief [vv.20–21]. This stunningly simple choice faces anyone who follows Jesus.

JOHN THE BAPTIST TELLS HIS DISCIPLES TO DELIGHT IN JESUS' TEACHING [JN.3:22–30]

²² Jesus and his disciples left Jerusalem and traveled around other parts of Judean territory. As they traveled, they baptized. ²³ At this time John was baptizing at Aenon near Salim. This was close to Samaritan territory. [The reasons the Baptist chose that place were plain:] there was an abundance of water in Aenon, and the people there sought baptism. ²⁴ This, of course, was before John's imprisonment. ²⁵ [While John was at Aenon,] a Jew there asked his disciples the purpose of their purification ritual. ²⁶ His disciples used this mention of baptism to tell John, "Teacher, the man who was at the Jordan when you were baptizing, the one you pointed out, is now also baptizing. And everybody's going to him." [27] *This is what John said in response: "Nothing happens to anyone unless it comes from God's plan.* [28] *You already heard what I said to others: 'I wasn't sent by God as God's Anointed One. I was sent ahead—before the anointed one' [see 1:30].* [29] *At a wedding, there's no argument who the groom is—he's the one with the bride! The groom's friend, on the other hand, is the one who stands there and, hearing what the groom declares, is delighted. When he hears the groom say what he has to say, his joy is complete.* [30] *Isn't it obvious? The one you're worried about must continue to increase. I must decrease."*

This abrupt shift back to John the Baptist might at first appear to change the subject from the lofty question of spiritual rebirth to procedural questions about purification rituals and who can perform them. Perhaps the question about baptism was asked of the Baptist's disciples [v.25] because word had spread that two groups were suddenly practicing it separately. Or we can suppose the query was similar to the troubled questions put to John by the authorities from Jerusalem [1:19–25]. Or the question might simply have meant: "What's the purpose of baptism?" But the question is never answered because the evangelist shows us the Baptist's disciples distracted by the fact that Jesus and his disciples were doing something that they apparently felt should be done only by their teacher, John [v.26].

But the evangelist also leaves unanswered the question: Why *was* Jesus baptizing? Instead, he describes the Baptist cutting through all the confusion [v.27] by speaking a variation of the modern cliché: "If something is of God, it will flourish; if not, it won't." And the answer contains an implicit question—a question for us as well as for his disciples: Do you think you understand God's ways? The Baptist seems to be asking his disciples to notice that they are anxious about their roles. We then hear him remind them that his role is to point out God's work, not his own work [v.28]. He uses the image of a wedding to say, "Notice the anointed one." Notice his works and delight in them, rather than in your own works [vv.29–30].

This scene between John and his disciples, like all those that precede it, depicts questioners who are puzzled or disturbed by someone's actions or words. Here, as in each former case, the questioners have been invited to ask themselves what they understand about God's desires. All the questioners (i.e., the officials from Jerusalem, who questioned the Baptist; the Baptist's disciples, who questioned Jesus; Jesus, who questioned Mary at Cana; the Jews who questioned Jesus after he cleansed the Temple; Nicodemus, questioning Jesus; and now the Baptist's disciples questioning him) have their questions turned back at them for reconsideration. They're forced to consider the possibility that God could be working to reveal and share his glory even where the questioner least expects it. Jesus accepted the possibility that God was at work in him at Cana. John has been portraying Jesus as the perfect student of God's way—and also the perfect teacher. Next, John comments on Jesus' unique qualifications to teach.

THE EVANGELIST COMMENTS ABOUT JESUS' WORDS
[JN.3:31–36]

31 Jesus comes from God, so we should obviously listen to him before any one else. The opposite is just as obvious: if someone is from this world, well, that one's bound to talk of earthly matters. So Jesus, coming from God, takes precedence. 32 Jesus speaks of God—about what he knows, what he's seen, what he's heard. But [I've already said it was shocking that we rejected the Word of God (1:10–11) and I'm saying it again:] no one received the witness of the one sent by God! 33 However, when you do receive his testimony, you're also giving testimony. You're testifying that you trust that God is telling the truth. 34 Because God's own Word is speaking, you can expect to hear the full outpouring of the divine truth—the very Spirit of God. 35 [There's no point in going further if you don't accept the following basic truth:] Because God the Father loves his only Son, he holds nothing back from him. He gives everything into his hands. 36 So, when you listen to what the Son speaks to you from the Father, you're taking in

God's own life, not just his words. On the other hand, if you don't accept the truth that the Son tells you—well, in that case, you've accepted the opposite of life. How dreadful is God's disappointment in you.

—————————

These comments offer another variation of the evangelist's basic message: God is trying to fill you with divine gifts. If we'd like to hear God speaking this truth to us, then we'll have to accept God's manner of speech. John says God has chosen to express his Word to us in Jesus [v.31]. Of course, if we're only interested in earthly matters, we'll keep listening only to earthbound experts. And if we think heavenly matters are simply an extension of earthly matters, we're likely to treat Jesus like any other source of earthbound information—we'll want to check his facts; we won't simply take him at his word [v.32]. The simplest way to resist Jesus is to regard him with the same wariness we bring to most encounters: we keep our distance and avoid the risk of getting involved. On the other hand, if we did embrace Jesus' message, and embrace it wholeheartedly, we would send a very strong message. We'd be saying to anyone paying attention to us that we believe Jesus' word is true [v.33].

The reason for doing this wholeheartedly is that one can't accept a little bit of God's gift to us because God's gift to us is himself—all that he is [v.34]. That's Jesus' message: God is pleased to share all he is with all his children. Jesus is the one child of God—the Son of Man—who truly believes that God is eager to give us divine life [v.35]. If you too want to share God's life, you'll follow the Son's example—you'll follow his whole way of living, his whole life. If you don't accept him—well, what do you have if you don't have divine life [v.36]?

FOUR

Acceptance by Samaritans; Acceptance by a Royal Official

A SAMARITAN WOMAN IS INVITED TO BELIEVE IN JESUS
[JN.4:1–26]

1 [As he traveled through Judea,] Jesus heard that the Pharisees back in Jerusalem had noticed that he was now baptizing—and was drawing more crowds and followers than John. 2 Some argued whether it was Jesus or his disciples who were baptizing. 3 Jesus decided to leave Judean territory. He traveled north, to Galilee. 4 His route took him through the area known as Samaria. 5 He stopped near a town called Sychar, which was next to the land that Jacob had given his son, Joseph. 6 Jacob's well was on that land. Jesus was tired when he got to the well, so he sat down and rested. It was midday. 7 A Samaritan woman came out to draw water from the well. Jesus asked for a drink. 8 (His disciples had gone into town for supplies.) 9 The woman said, "You're a Jew. You're asking me, a Samaritan, for a drink?" Ordinarily, Jews had nothing to do with Samaritans. 10 [Jesus ignored the differences in their belief, and focused instead on the basic question of what it means to believe.] Jesus said, "If you had any clear idea of how God wants to give you the divine gift—and if you had any idea who is asking you for a drink—you'd be doing the asking. He would, of course, give you the water of life." 11 "The well's deep and you don't have a bucket," said the woman. "Where are you going to get your 'water of life'? 12 Do you think you can find a

27

better source of water than this well? Our ancestor is Jacob, and he gave us this well. He drank its water. His children and his children's flocks drank this water." ¹³ *"Well," said Jesus, "anyone [yes, Jacob, his children, his descendants; yes, anyone] who takes a drink of this water will get thirsty again.* ¹⁴ *But anyone who drinks the water I can give will never thirst. The gift of water I'm talking about is the gush of eternal life."* ¹⁵ *"Go ahead, Mister," said the woman. "Give me this water. Then I won't get thirsty; I won't need to go back and forth from this well."* ¹⁶ *"Let's include your husband in this discussion," said Jesus. "Call him."* ¹⁷ *When she said, "I don't have a husband," Jesus said, "You can say that again.* ¹⁸ *You've had five husbands: and the one you're with now is no husband. You're telling the truth."* ¹⁹ *"Oh?" she said. "You know the truth? You're a prophet?* ²⁰ *Well, tell me this. Why did our ancestors worship God on this mountain, but your people insist that worshiping God has to happen in Jerusalem?"* ²¹ *"My dear," said Jesus, "the hour is at hand when people will most certainly turn to worship the Father—but neither on this mountain, nor in Jerusalem.* ²² *You Samaritans have forgotten how to turn to God [although the scriptures taught you]. We Jews have not forgotten. We know the source of our salvation.* ²³ *But now comes the hour (in fact, it's already here) when worshipers everywhere will turn to the Father and be filled with the Father's Spirit—with the Spirit of truth. The Father struggles constantly to inspire such worshipers.* ²⁴ *Because God inspires us as Spirit, we have to open ourselves to the Spirit's inspiration. God is revealing the whole truth to us about life—about divine life."* ²⁵ *The woman said, "I know the Messiah—the Anointed One from God—is supposed to come. I know he's supposed to reveal everything."* ²⁶ *"I am," said Jesus. "I am revealing everything to you."*

John doesn't tell us why a woman has come alone to the town well at an unusual hour. Neither does he describe her as ready for a conversation with a stranger about her deepest hopes: "If you only knew God's gift to you!" [v.10]. What he tells us is that she and Jesus offered conflicting opinions about their needs. The woman, at first, gives as good as she gets. She's honest about her domestic arrangements, and she's direct in her demand that, if Jesus is truly a prophet, he should be able to explain the Jewish-Samaritan schism.

But Jesus avoids a tit-for-tat exchange and gets to basic business. He says, in effect, "You know where scripture tells us to look for assurance: only to God [v.21]. You must ask yourself whether or not you truly expect this divine aid [v.22]. Do you think God's love and care for you is working right here, right now, at this moment [vv.23–24]?" John describes the woman as willing to admit she's heard something about a future Messiah, but unable to give any evidence of an active, present-tense faith in the divine promises. Notice how distant God is presumed to be. Despite God's repeated divine pledge—recorded in the scriptures—to be with us always, the woman's hope for divine care is placed in some vague future [v.25]. The reader who doesn't already know this story may assume that this woman, like most of the people Jesus has met so far, will continue to defer her hopes rather than believe right now. But then we hear Jesus tell her that's not necessary [v.26].

THE WOMAN GIVES WITNESS TO HER BELIEF [JN.4:27–30]

[27] *At that point, his disciples returned from their foray into town, surprised to find Jesus talking with this woman. However, none of them said, "What are you doing here?" or "What's going on?"* [28] *With her conversation interrupted, the woman suddenly left her bucket and went back to town. There, she started talking to all she met.* [29] *"Come," she said. "Come with me and meet a man who revealed my whole life to me. This could be the Messiah—God's own Anointed One."* [30] *People left the town and started off to see Jesus.*

Anyone making a film of this episode would have to decide how to dramatize the woman's moment of realization that Jesus might be the Messiah. To capture this woman's profound feelings, a film-maker might want to suggest that, though she was apparently baffled by Jesus' knowledge of her personal life, she was also surprised that he hadn't looked down on her for living the way she did. Instead, he had simply offered her a life that was more full, nourishing, and real. We'll have to wait for that film. Meanwhile, we have

John's description of her telling everyone she met that they should
share her experience of having their life revealed to them [v.29]. For
those with a past to hide, this might not have seemed like good
news. But this woman doesn't seem to be referring to the revelation
of the shameful (shameless?) life that was briefly outlined in the text
(see v.18). The life Jesus revealed to her was not her serial marriages
or sexual history. She needed no revelation to tell her what she
already knew. No, Jesus revealed to her that her life, which might
have seemed to be without hope, was actually filled with divine
light and life. John describes her giving witness to her belief in this
revelation and inviting the whole town to ask: Could God's
anointed be here with us? Is God fulfilling his promise to save us
right now?

Previously, John told us that if a person received Jesus' witness,
then that person was also giving witness (see 3:33). Here we have an
example of someone who takes in Jesus' message and then—apparently without regard for the amazement or censure of her neighbors—blurts it out.

JESUS VISITS THE WOMAN'S TOWN [JN.4:31–42]

*³¹ While all this was happening, Jesus' disciples were plying him with food.
"Teacher," they said, "eat!" ³² "I have food you don't know about," he said.
³³ "Where'd he get something to eat?" they wondered. ³⁴ "I'm fed by fulfilling my
Father's will," he told them. "I'm nourished by doing his work. [I mean, of course,
the Father's work of giving us divine life.] ³⁵ You say such things as, 'Only four
more months to harvest!' Well, look around. Here is a harvest abundant and
ready. ³⁶ Here—now, at this moment, as we speak—the harvester's been paid
and has started the harvest [of eternal life]. And the harvester of this crop is
working at the same time as the sower. [Amazing! Someone has made planting
and harvesting a one-step process—no waiting!] ³⁷ Here's the truth behind the
old saying, 'One sows, but someone else reaps.' ³⁸ [This is what I mean:] I sent
you to harvest what you haven't planted. Others prepared the harvest. [Our
Father, of course, is the creator of this abundance.] Now you get to rejoice in the
abundance."*

³⁹ *Many from Sychar put their trust in Jesus because the woman said, "He told me all about my life." ⁴⁰ When the Samaritans met him, they asked him to stay. And he did—two days. ⁴¹ During his stay, many others from the town put their trust in him because of what he taught them. ⁴² These new believers told the woman, "It's not just your word that makes us believe. We've heard him now ourselves, and we say that this is truly the savior of the world."*

⟝⟞⟝⟞⟝⟞

As John describes it, Jesus' playful way of speaking of nourishment may seem too pithy for comprehension [vv.32–34]. But the mention of the ease with which we humans tell one another what to expect from life—"In four months, the harvest!"—is a tipoff [v.35a]. Jesus is telling his followers that, if they can imagine a bumper crop for next season, they can also imagine the bounty God is producing right now [v.35b]. Look around, Jesus tells his disciples; it doesn't matter whether you see a crowd of strangers approaching from a Samaritan town or an unfamiliar person knocking at the door. Every human being is part of the bounty of eternal life [v.36a]—how blessed and lucky you are when you see that divine life bearing fruit and falling into your lap [v.36b]. John depicts Jesus telling his disciples that, if they would allow the Father to work for them, they'd be surprised by his abilities [vv.37–38]. Though John says nothing about the disciples' reaction to this image of a plentiful harvest, he does tell us the people from the town of Sychar gave signs of believing his description of God's powers [vv.39–41].

It might surprise some readers to read that the Samaritans called Jesus "savior of the world" [v.42]. But any reader who is puzzled by the title hasn't been paying attention to Jesus' words already cited for us in this Gospel. According to John, all Jesus' words and actions are focused on one thing: his relationship with the Father. What the Samaritans had heard and believed was Jesus' message about God: God is bent on freeing us from the dark and disquiet that roils our daily lives; he is determined to bring us to everlasting life—in a word, to save us. They couldn't have hit on a more apt title for the one who reveals this truth than "savior of the world." Although it shouldn't surprise us if some people who believe this life-saving message call Jesus a savior, it should startle us that so few others who've listened to Jesus believe his promise of salvation. John has already pointed out that Jesus' word wasn't accepted by his fellow Jews (e.g., 1:11; 3:32). His message that God is intent on filling them with eternal life was met with puzzlement and skepticism. John has now presented us with the irony that Jesus' first true believers were not Jews, but Samaritans.

BACK TO GALILEE; AN OFFICIAL BELIEVES JESUS BECAUSE OF A HEALING [JN.4:43–54]

[43] *After his two-day visit with the townspeople of Sychar, Jesus and his disciples continued on to Galilee.* [44] *[As they left Samaritan territory and headed back to Jewish territory,] Jesus couldn't help recalling the old saw that a prophet gets no hearing in his own country.* [45] *But back they went to Galilee. The Galileans recognized who he was because they remembered what he did when they were in Jerusalem for Passover.* [46] *Jesus traveled north in Galilee all the way to Cana, where he'd made the water wine. Almost twenty miles away, in Capernaum, there was a royal official [in the service of King Herod] whose son was mortally sick.* [47] *When the official heard that Jesus was back in Galilee, he went to Cana and asked Jesus to come down [to Capernaum on the Lake of Galilee] and heal his dying son.* [48] *Jesus said, "Belief for you people is always about signs and wonders."* [49] *But the official persisted: "My Lord, come with me before my boy dies."* [50] *Jesus said, "You can go on your own. Your son is well." The fellow believed him, so he left.* [51] *As the official was traveling back to Capernaum, his servants were traveling to meet him. The good news they gave him was that the boy was well.* [52] *When the official asked when this had happened, they said, "The fever broke yesterday around noon."* [53] *He knew that was when Jesus had told him, "Your son is well." The official and all his household became believers.* [54] *Twice now, Jesus has left Judea, gone to Galilee, and given a sign.*

—⟡—

Jesus' citation of an old adage about unheeded prophets suggests he was affected by the irony of succeeding with Samaritans but failing with fellow Jews. As he returns to Galilee [v.43], he's described as thinking, "Here we go, back to the usual crowd" [v.44]. For he was about to face the same group whose protests of belief he had mistrusted in Jerusalem [v.45; see 2:24–25]. However, even if we imagine that Jesus saw no difference between the royal official here seeking his help and the Galileans who were curious about some things he'd done in Jerusalem, we may nonetheless feel Jesus' words to the official are a harsh response to a frantic parent [v.48]. But John portrays Jesus spending no time on formalities that aren't essential to his work. And his work is not to satisfy human longings; his work is to satisfy God's longings. If that seems harsh, we should remember that this Gospel has been telling us that human needs are created and satisfied only by God—our true longings and God's are essentially the same!

In this scene, John tells us that Jesus insisted his mission wasn't to work wonders [v.48]. Nonetheless, Jesus does act miraculously—first, to help a bridegroom with no wine (see 2:11); now, to help a man with a sick son. But John isn't describing a contradiction in Jesus' behavior. The evangelist said from the beginning that God's Word comes into the world in order to shine divine light into our darkness [1:4–5], to make us aware of our status as God's children [1:12], to reveal God's glory to us [1:14], and to make us realize that God's fullness and grace are pouring into us [1:16]. As we've followed the encounters described by the Gospel so far, we've known—as the characters in these encounters could not have known—why Jesus spoke and acted as he did. His motives and intentions were disclosed to us in the introduction. But, despite that disclosure, we may still be puzzled by some of Jesus' words and actions. How much more baffling must it have been for those who encountered Jesus without the guidance of the evangelist. And yet, we're told that some who heard Jesus' message simply chose the pleasure of believing it rather than the strain of wrestling with bafflement. Jesus keeps telling all those willing to listen to him that, if they feel overwhelmed by such things as anger, anxiety, fear, re-

sentment, loneliness, and grief, they can be freed from their suffering. They can choose to believe that help, comfort, and release are at
hand. What Good News!

FIVE

Jerusalem Authorities Shocked by Jesus' Belief in His Relationship with the Father

JESUS HEALS A SICK MAN ON A SABBATH; PROTESTS
AGAINST THE HEALING [JN.5:1–16]

[1] *Later on, there was another Jewish feast, and Jesus went to Jerusalem to celebrate it.* [2] *In Jerusalem, there's a place called the Sheep Pool. The pool has colonnades along its sides and across the middle [forming two pools]. Its Hebrew name is Bethesda.* [3] *All along the colonnades lay a large number of the sick and disabled. They were hoping for healing from the water. [* [4] *A line explaining the pool's intermittent bubbling as the work of an angel is omitted by most manuscripts.]* [5] *One man lying there had been sick for thirty-eight years.* [6] *Jesus could tell he'd been sick a long time, and he asked him, "Do you want to be well?"* [7] *The man said, "Yes! But there's no one to help me to the pool when [the healing power of] the water's stirred up. When I try to manage on my own, I'm too late."* [8] *"Rise," Jesus said. "Take your mat and be on your way."* [9] *The man, now suddenly well, took his mat and walked away. It was the Sabbath.* [10] *"It's the Sabbath," said the Jews to the man who'd been healed. "It's against the law to carry a mat on the Sabbath."* [11] *"The man who made me well told me to take it with me."* [12] *"Who? Who told you to take it with you?"* [13] *The man who'd been made well didn't know the identity of Jesus—who had already disappeared in*

the crowd. ¹⁴ But, a while later at the Temple, Jesus encountered the man again. He said to him, "Notice that you've been healed [from your illness]. Now seek to be healed from sinfulness. Worse things can happen to you [than illness]." ¹⁵ The man went to the Jews and told them it was Jesus who made him well. ¹⁶ Because Jesus did this on a Sabbath, the Jews began to persecute and harass him.

————⟡⟡⟡————

I assume it's for dramatic effect that John holds back the information that it was the Sabbath [v.9b]. It's analogous to a crime writer setting a scene and then concluding the description by saying: "As those customers in the bank that morning went about their business, a man walked over to the manager. He was carrying a gun." Suddenly, we know there's going to be trouble. John assumes readers know that there were all sorts of laws to help keep the Sabbath sacred. Readers will also assume—from the prickly nature John has ascribed to the Jewish authorities—that a problem is likely to arise if someone breaks those laws.

Let's look at the moments that lead up to the authorities' opposition to Jesus [v.16]. First, Jesus was moved by the need of a sick man; second, the man showed no interest in Jesus' identity or motive; third, the Jewish authorities' only interest in the man's healing was that it broke the law. In the first moment, Jesus asked a man who'd been sick a long time if he wanted to be well [v.6]. (Try this question on a stranger the next time you visit a hospital, and see what reaction you get.) Jesus' blunt way of getting to the point here is similar to other examples of his direct address. He spoke frankly to his mother at Cana; he challenged Nicodemus's teaching qualifications; and he told the Samaritan woman she needed more than well water. Although Jesus' candor may seem almost rude, even callous, readers will know by now that he's interested in only one question. It's the first question—and the first words—attributed to Jesus in this Gospel: "What are you looking for?" [1:38]. Jesus was asking the sick man that question.

In the second moment of the scene, the sick man's response to Jesus' question was, essentially, "I've been looking for a cure, but I can't get one!" Like the woman at the well, this man seems puzzled—if not a little annoyed—by Jesus' words [v.7]. Unlike the woman's initial confusion, however, the sick man's bewilderment didn't yield to further curiosity and questions. His abrupt departure after his healing suggests he was simply glad to get on with life— the vigorous life he'd apparently been dreaming of for a long time [v.9]. A desire to get through life without trouble certainly seems to motivate his report of Jesus' identity to the authorities.

Third, John stresses the Jewish authorities' fixation on law and order. In a sense, they and the healed man were looking for the same thing: a hassle-free existence. The healed man wants to feel fit and avoid entanglements; the authorities want to get rid of a law-breaker. Although the text of the Gospel refers to "the Jews" rather than "the Jewish authorities" throughout this scene, it's clear that John doesn't mean all the Jews in Jerusalem—or all the Jews in Judea. He's talking about individuals who have the power to make and implement decisions. But before we judge the aggressive authorities too harshly, perhaps we should admit that everybody wants troublemakers off the street. We all think we know what kind of behavior would make our lives safer, easier, and happier. But, as we'll see, Jesus disagrees with this attitude.

JESUS DEFENDS HIS WORK AS GOD'S WORK [JN.5:17–30]

[17] Jesus explained [to the officials], "My Father's always at work. So, I'm at work." [18] The Jews thought he should be condemned to death for violating the Sabbath law and calling God "Father"—making himself equal to God; making himself a divine power! [19] [Defending his statement that his work came from the Father,] Jesus said, "O, yes; O, yes. O yes, indeed, I mean what I say. The Son doesn't act on his own. He watches what his Father does, and he follows his example—like father, like son. [20] In turn, because the Father loves the Son, he reveals all his work to him. And [because he's revealing all his work,] he'll reveal many more astonishing things than what you've just witnessed [in the healing of

a sick man. [21] What 'astonishing things'? You know that scripture says God controls life and death. In the book of Samuel, for example, we read, 'The Lord brings death and gives life. He allows a descent into darkness; he gives a return to life'; 1 Sam.2:6]. Now, just as the Father raises the dead and fills them with life, the Son also gives life to anyone he wants. [22] [You also know from scripture we must leave judgment to God. We read in Deuteronomy, for instance, 'Surely the Lord shall do justice for his people; he'll have pity on his servants'; Dt.32:36.] Now, the Father leaves all judgment to the Son. [23] [And why does the Father do this?] He does it so that everyone will revere and love the Son as they revere and love the Father. If you don't respect his Son, you can't possibly honor the Father who sends him to you. [24] O, yes; O yes. O yes, indeed, I'm saying that those who choose to take in my word, trusting that it comes from the Father, are choosing to take in divine life. No one can be condemned for making that choice. Those who make that choice are choosing life! [25] O, yes; O, yes. O yes, indeed, I say that the dead are now hearing the voice of God's Son—and the dead who accept that word are accepting life. [26] The Father is the source of all life. He shares his life-giving power with his Son. [27] The Father also shares with his Son the power of bringing justice, because he is the Son of Man [i.e., the Father is sharing his divine work with me, a human being, the Son of Man, just as he has always promised to share himself with us]. [28] Don't be shocked by what I've said. I'm not talking nonsense. Yes, the moment has come for the dead to hear the Son and rise to the sound of his voice. [29] The dead will come forward. Those who choose the right way will rise up to eternal life. Those who choose to follow their own wicked way to ruin will rise to ruin. [30] [So it's not true that I've claimed a power apart from God's. Nor am I competing with God for an independent, equal status; see v.18.] I don't do anything independently from the Father. My judgment is the judgment I hear from God. I'm not looking for a different way to see life. I want to see life as my Father sees it. I want what my Father wants."

—⟐⟐⟐—

Because of the concision of the text here, Jesus' words may seem enigmatic—even when they're read along with the references I've added. But John is describing Jesus making a simple point—and doing so here by using an image that everyone can follow. If a father and a son are to have a good relationship, it must be based on mutual openness and trust. A devoted son will feel free to imitate his father closely; and a loving father will not keep secrets from his son. (The maleness of the father-son imagery needn't obscure Jesus' plain truth: we expect the relationship between parents and their children to be honest, open, and generous. Cinderella and Harry Potter elicit our sympathy, for example, because their relatives refuse to offer this kind of relationship.) John is portraying Jesus, a Jew, speaking to his fellow Jews about a relationship they all share: they are children of God. If the Jews who questioned the propriety of Jesus healing on a Sabbath truly believed in this relationship, none of them would have found it odd or offensive that Jesus not only called God "Father" but also felt free to imitate his Father's famous divine care—for instance, by healing a sick man. But they will be surprised, says Jesus, when they see more astonishing things than the healing of a single man.

Here Jesus is restating basic Jewish belief. He could have cited Genesis: "God created human beings in his image; in the divine image he created them; male and female he created them" [Gen.1:27]. And then he could have added, "Of course I behave like God. How else would I behave—I'm made in his image!" Instead, John lets Jesus speak more succinctly: "The Father returns the dead to life, and so will I. The Father judges mercifully, and so will I" [vv.21–22]. One reason Jesus' listeners might have been confounded by these statements is that they kept thinking of life as they knew it. But Jesus speaks of life as God knows it.

The scriptures tell us over and over that God desires to make his children full heirs to divine life. But the scriptures also tell us that God's children repeatedly refused to trust God's desire. Starting with the story of Adam and Eve, we're told that human beings have constantly tried to wrest control of life from God and take charge of it themselves. Each effort has ended in misery. But, according to the Bible, after each failed human attempt to break away from God, God repaired the relationship. God judged that, when his children sinned (i.e., refused to share his life), it would be good to rescue them from their deadly choice. If Jesus believes that he is truly the Son of God, of course he'll be like his Father. He'll keep offering divine life to those who've turned away from it and chosen "death." He'll keep offering justice—showing the right way—to those who've lost the way. In other words, when you see Jesus' life-giving actions, you see the work of the Father [v.23].

John then describes Jesus pointing out the obvious conclusion to what he's been saying. People who are interested in shaping their lives by themselves—that is, those who turn away from the Father's creative work and trust their own ingenious schemes—will achieve nothing. We hear Jesus call this state of nothingness "death," but he's not speaking about the dying that's a natural part of everyone's life [vv.24–25]. He's referring to the deadly decision to annihilate God's presence from one's life. Then, says John, Jesus reviewed the points he'd made.

The description of Jesus repeating previous statements suggests a wish to leave no confusion: Jesus' desires, aims, and works were the same as the Father's. It was important that his listeners understand he wasn't reaching for divine power, but that divine power was given to him. As he said at the beginning of his response to his accusers, in an ideal relationship between a father and son, the son is glad to take on the father's work and finish it faithfully. And, if the father is truly loving, he'll be happy to see his work completed by his son. Jesus' human experiences have confirmed his belief that the Father wants the perfect relationship described in the scriptures. So, as the one human being who fully accepts God's promises as true—as the Son of Man—he's confident that the Father shares divine power with him. Jesus won't now deny that relationship merely because the authorities seem offended by the notion of it [vv.26–30].

JESUS CONTINUES TO DEFEND HIS RELATIONSHIP WITH THE FATHER [JN.5:31–47]

[31] *[Jesus was speaking to the authorities.] "If I speak for myself, I have no corroborating witness.* [32] *But I have a witness to testify for me; and I know that the testimony given is true.* [33] *You asked John for the truth, and he gave it to you.*

³⁴ No, I'm not saying that he's my witness. I don't need a human witness. I only mention John to point out that even a human voice, like John's, can help save someone from closed-mindedness. ³⁵ John blazed like a lamp. And, for a moment, you were fascinated by his brightness. ³⁶ But my witness is greater than John. My witness is the work the Father has given me to complete. Yes, I'm talking about the work you say I have no right to claim. The divine works that I'm accomplishing give witness that it's the Father who is at work. He sent me to do his work. ³⁷ But these works are not the only witness. The Father himself is also my witness. True, you haven't heard him or seen him. ³⁸ But that's because you haven't taken his word—the scriptures—to heart. [How do I know this?] You don't believe his word when you hear it from the one he sent! ³⁹ Yes, you rummage through the scriptures thinking you'll get a grip on eternal life. But don't you notice that the scriptures contain the Father's witness about me? ⁴⁰ You want eternal life, but you won't come to me! ⁴¹ I'm not looking for praise and admiration from mortals. ⁴² [You, however, do want worldly glory.] Your hearts don't yearn for God's glory. ⁴³ I came to you in my Father's name. [It shouldn't surprise you that God—who has always loved you and is always speaking to you—would send me to bring you good news.] But you don't accept me. And yet you'll listen to anyone who strikes you as important. ⁴⁴ How will you ever learn to believe [in God] if all your enthusiasm is for other self-glorifying human beings— if you have no desire for the glory of the one, true God? ⁴⁵ I'm not accusing you falsely before God. It's Moses who makes the accusation—Moses, in whose word you supposedly place such confidence. ⁴⁶ If you truly believed Moses, you'd believe me. He was writing about me! [Yes, he wrote about the sort of prophet who speaks the word of God—God's words, not his own.] ⁴⁷ But if you don't believe Moses, how will you believe what I say?"

—❧❧❧—

The evangelist describes Jesus making his point in careful, simple steps in order to help the authorities see two familiar things in a way that has escaped them. First, they know they prize the unique relationship between a parent and a child. They also know that scripture assures them they are children of God. Put these two truths together, and you've learned to recognize the perfect relationship. According to John, Jesus seemed to think that, if his listeners understood this lesson, they'd accept his statement that he does his Father's work (no one's surprised when a son goes into the family business) [vv.31–37a]. But apparently the authorities refuse to imagine that such a close connection can exist between Jesus and God, their Father. Jesus has encountered a teacher's worst nightmare: a case of invincible ignorance [vv.37b–40]. Although he gives his listeners a second example to help them understand the intimate bond between God and his children (asking them to consider the difference between the glory we can create for ourselves, and the glory God wants to share with us [vv.41–44]), he doesn't sound too hopeful that they will ever truly listen [vv.45–47]. Next, we'll hear that Jesus has left Jerusalem for more travels.

SIX

Jesus Scandalizes His Fellow
Galileans with the Gift of Himself

BY GIVING THANKS TO GOD, JESUS FEEDS
A HUNGRY CROWD [JN.6:1–15]

[1] *Jesus' travels took him to the other side of the Sea of Galilee.* [2] *A large crowd dogged his footsteps because they'd seen the signs he accomplished with the sick.* [3] *Jesus kept moving, and headed up Mount Pleasant where he rested with his disciples.* [4] *This was just before the Passover feast.* [5] *When Jesus saw that the crowds had followed him up the mountain, he asked Philip, "Where can we get enough bread so they can eat?"* [6] *Jesus asked Philip this question to see what he'd learned. He already knew what he himself would do.* [7] *Philip said, "If we had two hundred denarii—more than a man is paid for half a year's work— we couldn't buy enough for everyone to have a nibble."* [8] *Andrew, the brother of Simon "Peter" [and one of Jesus' first disciples], spoke up.* [9] *"There's a young one here who has five loaves of cheap barley bread and a couple of salted fish. But what's that? There are so many!"* [10] *Jesus said, "Get everyone to settle down." There was plenty of grassy ground on which people could spread out. The men in the crowd of about five thousand settled and arranged people into groups.* [11] *Jesus took the cheap barley loaves, gave thanks to the Father, and sent them around to the groups on the grass. He also sent around the fish—as much as anyone cared for.* [12] *After they finished eating, Jesus told his disciples,*

43

"Go get what's left over. We don't want to waste anything." [13] *After the crowd had eaten, the disciples collected enough leftovers to fill twelve baskets.* [14] *When the crowd saw what had happened, they agreed it was a sign. "There's no doubt. This is the Prophet promised in the scriptures" [Dt.18:15; see above 1:21, 45].* [15] *Jesus could see what was happening. They wanted a powerful king who would bring them prosperity [not a true prophet who brought God's word]. He wasn't going to let himself be carried off by that notion. He retreated farther up the mountain.*

———

John doesn't name the spot Jesus climbed to with his friends. He simply writes, "the mountain." But I don't think the reader is meant to picture Jesus wandering aimlessly. No, he was headed to an out-of-the-way spot whose name is now lost to us—say, "Mt. Pleasant." However, we're told that, when Jesus arrived at this peaceful place, he didn't find peace. Instead, he was pursued by a crowd who, far from home, needed to eat [v.5]. And he wondered what his disciples made of this need. Their response to the question of how the hungry crowd might be fed is typically flat-footed [vv.6–9]. It echoes the bewildered responses Jesus has received before: How can one be born anew? How can one receive living water? How can one become well? Indeed, how are such things possible? First, everyone should settle down [v.10].

The sensible and worldly-wise disciples knew that feeding thousands of people was beyond their capabilities. And for them, that was the end of the matter. Jesus, however, is not worldly-wise. Human insight and wisdom are too limited for his needs. So he calls upon heaven—his Father. John's mention of Jesus' thanksgiving is so cursory that a reader might miss it. The succinct statement that Jesus "gave thanks" [v.11] reveals what Jesus "knew he would do" [v.6]—he was going to turn to the Father. At this point in the Gospel, we should recognize this as Jesus' instinctive impulse. In fact, turning to the Father is the only thing Jesus does—the only thing he's been trying to teach others to do. He told the Jerusalem authorities that he had no agenda but the Father's [5:19]. But not only has he consistently chosen to let God work in him, he's also been puz-zled when others don't make the same choice. If God wants to work in you, why would you prevent that work?

According to John, Jesus has been trying—and failing—to find out why his fellow Jews, including his disciples, don't instinctively turn to the Father to thank him for his care and to ask for more of it. Jesus seems baffled by their lack of common sense. After all, people often put praise in the form of a request. For example, when we tell the cook, "Thank you; it's delicious—may I please have some more," we not only say we're grateful, we also show our gratitude by asking for more. Jesus prays as someone who is delighted that his Father wants to serve him—wants to answer his prayer. His prayer is the same that any of his fellow Jews could pray. We could pray it as well. If the words didn't impulsively leap to our lips, we could borrow the words of a Psalm—say, Psalm 136. It begins with these three verses: "Give thanks to the Lord. He is good. His love is forever. / Give thanks to the Lord. He is good. His love is forever. / Give thanks to the Lord. He is good. His love is forever" [Ps.136:1–3].

If that prayer isn't clear enough for us, we could recast it in direct address. Say: "Thank you, God. You're so generous to me; give me your love always." It would be natural for Jesus, a devout Jew, to pray with such words. If we did the same, we would not only be acknowledging God's gift of love, we would also be con-fessing that we will always need it. But giving thanks for God's love wasn't the impulse of the well-fed crowd. Jesus' wonder-working was what they wanted [vv.14–15]. If Jesus was hoping that the crowd—and, perhaps, his disciples—would learn that his works, or "signs," were the Father's works, he was once again disappointed.

JESUS TELLS HIS DISCIPLES THERE'S NO NEED TO FEAR
[JN.6:16–21]

[16] As evening came on, the disciples descended from the mountain to the sea-shore. [17] They boarded their boat and headed for Capernaum. Darkness fell.

Jesus wasn't with them. ¹⁸ A strong wind kept up a constant chop. ¹⁹ Their rowing had taken them several miles when they saw Jesus walking toward them on the sea. They were frightened. ²⁰ "It's me," said Jesus. "No need to fear." ²¹ They wanted to get him aboard—but, suddenly, they were ashore.

This brief sequence of actions seems to break the rules of storytelling. If the author were pitching it as part of a film script, he could expect producers to protest, "Wait. Why did Jesus stay behind? Where were the disciples going on their own? Shouldn't somebody say something like, 'See you back at Capernaum'? What did the disciples make of being ashore so suddenly?" If we have similar questions, we're demonstrating a concern that's typical of Jesus' listeners: Why does Jesus do the things he does? But just as the disciples should have begun to learn the answer to this question, so should we. Jesus does what he does in order to let the Father work in him. If his witness to God's work—to God's ever-present care—is true, then we shouldn't have to keep checking repeatedly to make sure God is attending to us. Whether we're separated from friends, working in the dark, rowing against the wind, or simply baffled by something, we need not fear. That's Jesus' simple reminder to his disciples: "Don't be afraid" [v.20].

But people don't usually give up their questions, concerns, worries, and fears without a struggle. The crowd's struggle to make Jesus address their questions and concerns continues in the next scene.

THE WELL-FED CROWD WANTS FREE FOOD, NOT DIVINE FOOD [JN.6:22–35]

²² In the morning, the crowd woke after spending the night on the mountain [and found Jesus gone]. They knew the disciples had only one boat, and that they'd left without Jesus. ²³ There were other boats offshore where the crowd had been fed—fed because the Lord had given thanks. ²⁴ So when it was clear that the disciples and Jesus were no longer there, the crowd hailed the boats and sailed to Capernaum to look for Jesus. *²⁵ When they tracked him down [outside the synagogue], they said, "Teacher, when did you get here?" ²⁶ "O, yes; O, yes. O yes, indeed, let me tell you you're not looking for me because you saw [divine] signs," said Jesus, "but because you ate your fill of food. ²⁷ Don't work for perishable food. Struggle for the food of eternal life. That's the food the Son of Man will give you. Yes, the Father's promise [of eternal care] is guaranteed through the Son of Man." ²⁸ "How can we accomplish what God wants us to accomplish?" they asked Jesus. ²⁹ "What God wants you to do," said Jesus, "is believe in the one he sends you." ³⁰ They said, "What sign can you give us so we can believe in you? What can you accomplish? ³¹ Our ancestors ate manna [a sign from God!] during their time in the wilderness. It's in scripture: 'Bread will fall from heaven' [Ex.16:4]." ³² "O, yes; O, yes," said Jesus. "O yes, indeed, I know they received bread—but not from Moses. My Father in heaven gives true bread. ³³ God's bread is divine food for this world." ³⁴ "Well, then, Lord," they said, "keep giving us that bread." ³⁵ "I am the bread of life," said Jesus. "If you come to me, you'll never be hungry. If you believe in me, you'll never thirst."*

—◦◦◦—

The crowd finds Jesus in or near the synagogue (see below, 6:59). But, as John tells it, they weren't looking for a teacher, and Jesus knew it. The crowd was pleased by a performance and was hoping for an encore. However, Jesus didn't feed them to impress them with his power. It was to remind them of the power of God. That's why he gave thanks before he fed them (see 6:11). John helps the reader recall Jesus' prayer to the Father—a prayer the crowd apparently ignored—when he reminds us that the crowd was fed because "the Lord had given thanks" [v.23]. The reader knows that this "Lord" is the one who is the embodiment of God's Word. The crowd, however, regards Jesus as "Lord" because he fits their notion of "king." So we hear him tell them they seek him for the wrong reason. Then, as a patient teacher, Jesus invites them—just as he invited the woman at the well—to raise their expectations.

We can imagine the crowd thinking their expectations were high. They might have hoped to experience something like the miraculous supply of flour and oil that Elijah promised the starving widow of Zarephath [1 Kgs.17:14–16]. They seem to think that life is a struggle for the things of this world [v.31]. Meanwhile, Jesus was inviting them to imagine that life is all about God's struggle to give them divine glory [vv.32–33]. What did they make of Jesus' reply when they asked for God's food [vv.34–35]?

THE CROWD WON'T BELIEVE JESUS' OFFER TO FEED THEM TRUE BREAD [JN.6:35–51]

[35] *Jesus said to the crowd that had been fed, "I am the bread of life. If you come to me, you'll never be hungry. If you believe in me, you'll never thirst.* [36] *Now, I've said that, even though you've seen me [doing divine signs; see v.26], you don't believe.* [37] *Nonetheless, all that the Father gives to me will come to me. And I will not turn away a single person who comes to me.* [38] *I haven't come from the Father to do what I want. I come to do what he wants.* [39] *The Father, who sent me, wants this: that I let go of nothing he gives me. Instead, he wants me to bring everyone to life on the last day.* [40] *Yes, this is indeed what my Father wants. [So I'll say it again.] Anyone who comes to know the Son and puts faith in him has eternal life. That person I will raise on the last day."* [41] *The Jews grumbled with disapproval because they heard him say, "I'm bread from heaven."* [42] *They said, "Isn't this man Jesus? Isn't he Joseph's son? We know his father and mother! So, how can he say, 'I'm from heaven'?"* [43] *Jesus said, "Stop muttering to one another.* [44] *Of course you won't be interested in my teaching unless my Father, who sent me with the message, is the one who attracts you. The person who is attracted to the Father I will raise on the last day.* [45] *Read what the prophet wrote: 'They'll be taught by God' [Is.54:13]. If you listen to God teaching you—if you learn from my Father—you'll come to me.* [46] *I know that none of you has actually seen the Father. But I am from the Father. I have seen him.* [47] *O, yes; O, yes. O yes, indeed, I tell you that whoever believes this has eternal life.* [48] *I am the bread of everlasting life.* [49] *[Remember what you just told me:] Your ancestors ate manna in the desert [see v.31]. But they died.* [50] *If you eat this heavenly bread, you will not die.* [51] *I am the life-giving bread that comes from heaven. If you eat this bread, you live forever. The life-giving bread for this world is my flesh."*

—⟨υ/υ/υ⟩—

The first statements that John describes here could be said by any good teacher who believes God's offer of the Covenant as it's described in the scriptures. This ideal good teacher might say the following. "The truth I proclaim about God's promise to make us his children forever is life's true nourishment and, if you accept this truth, it will sustain you at all times [v.35]. But you're not accepting it [v.36]. However, anyone who *is* moved by the Father's Spirit to accept it will desire it—and I can't turn away from anyone with such a desire [v.37]. That's because I don't decide how things should be done—God does [v.38]. God, who inspires me to proclaim what I believe, is determined to leave no one out of this relationship—that is, the Covenant. Yes, he will bring divine life to all [v.39]. God deeply desires that the truth I'm proclaiming about his plan for you will be affirmed by your rising at the end of time" [v.40].

The only detail from verses 35–40 that I've left out of this paraphrase is the bracketed reference above to "divine signs" [v.36]—a detail that isn't in the Greek text of the Gospel. The Gospel text reads: "I've told you that you've seen but not believed." However, I think it's obvious that Jesus is referring to what the crowd saw him accomplish on the mountain—that is, a sign of God's care for their need. So everything Jesus is described saying here is either a truth proclaimed by scripture or a reference to the previous day. There's nothing in these words that his listeners should find objectionable. Nonetheless, they objected [vv.41–42]. Then, once again, Jesus is described asking listeners what they want—what they actually believe. If they believed in a God who created them as his own children and wanted them to share his own life, then they should be delighted with Jesus' news—the Good News that God has now sent his divine Son to bring them fully into their Father's life [vv.44–47]. If they truly believed scripture, Jesus' words would feed and deepen that belief. Because Jesus has been hoping to deepen their faith, he kept teaching them—kept asking them to reexamine their claim to believe. Did they think, for instance, that when Moses and the prophets spoke of God's promise to guide and protect his people, the promise was merely an assurance that he would send an endless supply of prophets? Or, as John the Baptist tried to point out (see 1:26), hadn't God promised to send someone greater than a prophet? Did they think the gift of manna was the extent of God's power? Or can they imagine that God's desire to give them his life might express itself in a more profound and lasting way [vv.49–51]?

JESUS PLEADS WITH THE CROWD TO LET HIM
FEED THEM PROPERLY [JN.6:51–59]

[51] [Jesus was still talking to the crowd that had been fed.] "I am the life-giving bread that comes from heaven. If you eat this bread, you live forever. The life-giving bread for this world is my flesh." [52] The Jews started arguing with one another about Jesus' meaning. "How can he give us his flesh to eat?" [53] "O, yes; O, yes. O yes, indeed, I am saying that if you don't eat the Son of Man's flesh and drink his blood, there's no life in you. [54] But those who do eat my flesh and drink my blood have everlasting life. I will raise them [to everlasting life] on the last day.

[55] My flesh is what's really food; my blood is what's truly drink. [56] Those who eat my flesh and drink my blood are one with me. [57] [I'm assuring you that] I'm from the Father, who lives eternally. It's the Father who gives me life. Anyone who feeds on me will therefore have the same life. [58] This bread [of divine life] comes from God. Yes [I'll say it again], your ancestors ate manna from God, but they died. But whoever eats this bread will live eternally." [59] Jesus did all this teaching at the Capernaum synagogue.

—◦◦◦—

Although John has described Jesus working intensely to get his point across to the crowd, they seem unwilling to explore or reimagine their beliefs. Consider, for example, their question, "How can he give us his flesh to eat?" [v.52]. If it's a rhetorical question—if they're not bloody-minded literalists asking how they should bite into Jesus—then it merely suggests they're refusing to imagine the possibility of absorbing Jesus wholly and entirely. They were assuming their way of understanding life was the only way to understand it. They seem to expect Jesus to defend his statement. But, at the same time, they seem unwilling to reflect seriously on the statement. Instead, their instant judgment is dismissive. Yet Jesus, still the hopeful teacher, continued his attempt to open their closed minds, warning them that, without his flesh and blood [v.53], they would have no life. Do we suppose the people in this scene should have been able to imagine a way in which it would be possible for them to take in Jesus completely—his flesh and his blood—and share his life perfectly? We who are reading this Gospel today know the end of the story; we know that, in dying on the cross, Jesus gave up this life of flesh and blood so that God could raise him to everlasting life. We know that, in the Eucharist, believers proclaim they are the Body of Christ—they share his death and resurrection. Does it seem that Jesus was expecting too much from listeners who don't know the rest of the story?

EVEN SOME DISCIPLES REFUSE JESUS' OFFER [JN.6:60–71]

⁶⁰ *[Some disciples who were listening to Jesus speak of giving his flesh to eat said,] "This is insane. Who can believe it?"* ⁶¹ *Jesus knew what they were muttering about. So he asked, "Does this affront you?* ⁶² *Would you also be shocked if you saw the Son of Man ascending to where he was before?* ⁶³ *Tell me this. Isn't it the Spirit that animates you? Isn't your flesh dependent on the Spirit? I've been speaking to you about God's Spirit—about life.* ⁶⁴ *But some of you don't believe what I'm saying." From the first, Jesus had known who would not believe—who would turn away from him.* ⁶⁵ *"But," he said, "you won't follow me unless the Father inspires you to do so."* ⁶⁶ *Because these disciples were baffled, they went away and no longer followed him.* ⁶⁷ *"Do you also want to go?" Jesus asked his twelve closest disciples.* ⁶⁸ *Simon "Peter" said, "Lord, where would we go? You speak of eternal life.* ⁶⁹ *We're starting to believe—in fact, we do believe—you're the Holy One of God."* ⁷⁰ *Jesus [challenging this declaration about the belief of the group] said, "I called the twelve of you. But one of you is driven by the devil."* ⁷¹ *He was talking about Judas Iscariot who, though one of the twelve, would betray him.*

—⸙⸙⸙—

According to John, Jesus didn't let his troubled disciples slink away
with the rest of the crowd without repeating his basic question
about belief: Did they believe their Father's promise to bring them
to eternal life? If they did believe in God's promise, would they
criticize God's method for fulfilling it? We hear him try to help
them with the same sort of image he offered Nathanael (see 1:51).
Can they imagine the Son of Man—a human like themselves—intimately joined with heaven [v.62]? Apparently some of them could
not [v.64].

When we read Jesus' description of Judas [v.70], we don't have
to suppose it sprang from knowledge of the future. What's important in his response to Peter's protestation of faith [vv.68–69] is not
whether it comes from Jesus' clairvoyance, but whether or not Jesus
expected Peter to see it as a challenge. If Peter had been paying
attention, he should have understood it. Jesus' assurance that he
was proclaiming his Father's truth and was doing the Father's work
has often met with puzzlement, skepticism, and outright contempt.
What makes Peter think he's not like the skeptics? What makes him
think his belief and that of the other disciples is genuine? Jesus has
told them that the Father—the Father who creates them, makes
them his children, and struggles to raise them to glory—is the one
who will inspire them to believe Jesus. Does Peter understand this?
Is he allowing the Father to put him completely into the hands of
Jesus? Readers familiar with the rest of the story know that Peter
hasn't entrusted himself to Jesus—does not yet believe.

SEVEN

In Jerusalem, Jesus Again Proclaims God Is the Only Source of Life

JESUS REJECTS WORLDLY SUCCESS; IN JERUSALEM, HE TEACHES SCRIPTURE [JN.7:1–31]

¹ Jesus continued to travel around Galilee. He wanted to avoid Judea. Remember that the Jewish authorities there were planning to kill him [see 5:18]. ² However, the Jews were about to celebrate the Feast of Tabernacles. [This feast recalled that, in the wilderness, when the people of God lived in tents, or "tabernacles," God was always with them.] ³ Jesus' brothers said, "Let's go down to Judea [for the feast]. Your disciples [in Jerusalem] should see your works. ⁴ You shouldn't work secretly if you want your work known. If you're going to do what you're doing, you should let the world know it." ⁵ His brothers had no faith in him. ⁶ Jesus told them, "This isn't the right moment for me. You, however, grab every moment you can. ⁷ The world likes your attitude. It despises mine because I call the selfishness of the world evil. ⁸ Go to the feast yourselves. This isn't the time for what I have to do." ⁹ So he stayed in Galilee. ¹⁰ Only after his brothers left for the feast did Jesus leave—secretly, if you will. ¹¹ At the feast, the Jewish authorities were looking for him: "Where is that one?" ¹² The crowd also talked about him. Some said he was a good man, others said he was a charlatan. ¹³ But no one in the crowd spoke publicly. They were afraid of the authorities.

¹⁴ In the middle of the feast, Jesus went into the Temple and taught. ¹⁵ The authorities were baffled. "He's never studied," they said. "How does he know scripture so well?" ¹⁶ "I'm not teaching what I know," said Jesus, "but what the one who sent me knows. ¹⁷ If you want what God wants, you'll know whether I speak for God or for myself. ¹⁸ Those who glorify themselves want the world to applaud whatever they do. But anyone seeking divine glory wants only [divine] truth. You can't go wrong with that! ¹⁹ Moses [yes, Moses, whom you so revere] gave you the law to act on. But you don't do it! Instead, you're trying to undo me—to kill me." ²⁰ "A demon's got hold of you!" said people in the crowd. "Who wants to kill you?" ²¹ [Jesus then reminded them of the fuss about his Sabbath healing; see 5:6–15.] He said, "Everyone was shocked when I did work on the Sabbath. ²² But look, Moses [yes, Moses !] passed on the practice of circumcision from our ancestors. And you perform circumcisions on the Sabbath. ²³ So, you'll circumcise someone on the Sabbath in order to adhere strictly to the Mosaic law, but you're furious with me because I healed someone on the Sabbath. ²⁴ Stop judging what you think you see. Learn the right way to judge." ²⁵ Some in Jerusalem said, "Isn't this the one they want to kill? ²⁶ Yet no one stops him from speaking in public. Maybe the authorities think he's the Messiah." ²⁷ "But we know where he's from," said some. "When the Messiah comes, no one will know his origins." ²⁸ Jesus called out to all in the Temple, "O, so you know me? You know my origins? I'm not talking about me and my origins! I'm speaking for the one who sent me—the one who knows all truth. But you don't realize who he is. ²⁹ I do know him. I am from him. He sent me." ³⁰ [These words were just the sort of talk that infuriated the authorities during Jesus' last Jerusalem visit. Now, once again, they become angry.] They looked for a way to arrest him. But no one made a move to do so—because the hour [for the completion of his divine work] had not yet come. ³¹ And some in the crowd were moved to believe in him. "When the Messiah comes," they said, "do you think he'll do more signs than this one?"

━━━∽∾∿∾∽━━━

The opening of this section emphasizes the failure of Jesus' teaching: first, we're reminded that his fellow Jews didn't merely reject his words, they also wanted to execute him for blasphemy [v.1]; then we're told that his close relatives had no faith in his teaching, but were eager for him to make an impression as a wonder-worker [vv.3–5]; finally, it appears as if Jesus didn't think a feast celebrating God's devotion to his people was the right moment to proclaim his message—the message that proclaims God's devotion to his children [v.6]. But Jesus' mention here of the right time or "moment" for him to work should remind readers of a similar remark to his mother at Cana. He's saying it's never the right time for him to show off—as his brothers wanted him to do. So of course he refused their invitation. However, he's not saying he has lost interest in teaching or doing the Father's work.

Incidentally, John's use of the Greek word for "brothers" indicates that, though Jesus was not talking with disciples, he was nonetheless speaking with individuals who, as relatives, might reasonably be supposed to know him well. And yet, they did not. When John says that even Jesus' "brothers" lacked faith, he highlights the loneliness of Jesus' position. He's not concerned with the specifics of Jesus' family tree, but with the fact that not even Jesus' close relatives seemed to understand his mission.

When John describes Jesus heading to Jerusalem alone, he indicates that the tension and stress that have permeated most of Jesus' teaching moments were again present [vv.10–13]. The fears and anxieties of his fellow Jews make them apt candidates for his Good News—that is, for this message: "Do not be afraid." But just as the healed man at the Sheep Pool allowed worry and dread to enslave him (see 5:7ff.), many in the crowd at this Feast of Tabernacles will let their prejudices keep them from hearing Jesus.

The answer to the question of how Jesus knows the scriptures without being a recognized scholar [vv.14–15] is quite simple. He paid attention when scripture was read—say, in the synagogue. We hear Jesus appealing to his listeners to believe that he is sent by God. He argues that they should believe his word for the same reason they believe the scriptures: you can't go wrong with the word of God [v.18]. The truth of God's power, care, and glory are revealed in the words of scripture, and Jesus is repeating that message—a message sent by God.

Then we hear Jesus offer a lesson from scripture to point out to the crowd that, although they have laws to help them remember that God has created them in the divine image, they don't live as though they believe this. When he says that, even on a Sabbath, they do the work of scarring the male body with a mark to signify "I belong to God," he is asking them why God couldn't also be working on the Sabbath in the healing of a sick man [vv.21–24]. Though Jesus' question provokes a confused response [vv.25–27], his lesson seems to have unsettled some of his listeners' prejudices. There may have been many in the crowd who shared the authorities' desire to have Jesus arrested because of his claim that his mission and his very being were from God [vv.29–30]. But John says some people had the impulse to believe Jesus because they were impressed by his signs—"Whenever the Messiah comes, will he do more signs than this one?" [v.31]. Note, however, that John doesn't mention here any earlier signs or miracles, nor has he described miracles performed during this visit to Jerusalem. The positive response of some in the crowd seems to be as much the result of the boldness of Jesus' teaching as a reaction to whatever they may have heard about his "signs."

This, the first part of Jesus' visit to the Temple during the Feast of Tabernacles, is like most of the previous teaching moments in the Gospel: Jesus offers a simple lesson, then there's a negative reaction by some, and a tentatively positive reaction by others.

THE AUTHORITIES WANT JESUS ARRESTED; PEOPLE STILL LISTEN [JN.7:32–36]

[32] *When the Pharisees heard how the crowd argued about Jesus, they and the chief priests sent the Temple guard to take him into custody.* [33] *[Nonetheless, Jesus continued to speak.] He said, "I am with you only briefly. I'm going to the one who sent me.* [34] *You'll look, but not find me. Where I am, you can't come."* [35] *"Where's he going that we can't find him?" they asked one another. "Is he going to far-off lands to teach those who speak Greek?"* [36] *And they asked,*

"What are all these riddles—'you'll look but not find'; and 'where I am, you can't come'?"

———∽∾∾∾———

John describes a crowd that can't seem to listen to Jesus with an open mind. They profess to be utterly puzzled by his mention of coming and going, seeking and finding. Despite Jesus' obvious grasp of scripture and the simple examples with which he has tried to bring scripture alive for his listeners, John says the Jewish authorities and most of the crowd continued to misunderstand him. Jesus might as well have been speaking a different language. That point is even glanced at jokingly when someone in the crowd makes the facetious remark that Jesus might try his teaching on Greek-speaking Jews [v.35]. Amid all the hubbub, argument, confusion, and complaining, Jesus' simple lesson is lost. He's saying that, because he's from God, God is with him in all his comings and goings. The crowd has trouble imagining that this Good News also applies to them. Instead, they trust they're clever enough to answer all their own questions—a process that can never result in good news. However, part of Jesus' message—and the message of scripture—is that God keeps speaking the truth even to those who refuse to listen. Therefore, Jesus doesn't stop teaching.

JESUS SAYS HE'S THE SOURCE OF LIVING WATER; SOME BELIEVE, SOME DON'T [JN.7:37–53]

37 On the climactic, last day of the feast, Jesus stood up once again. He called out, "If you thirst, come to me and drink. 38 If you believe in me, remember the promise of scripture: 'From the depth of his being springs living water.'" 39 Jesus was talking about the divine Spirit that would inflame believers with new life when he was glorified [after finishing his work]. 40 Some who heard Jesus' words said, "This is really the Prophet [promised by scripture; Dt.18:15; see above, 1:21, 45; 6:14]." 41 "This is the Messiah," said others. But others said, "You can't expect the Messiah to come from Galilee! 42 Scripture says the Messiah will come from David's family, from Bethlehem, where David lived." 43 Dissension swirled

*all around him. ⁴⁴ Some even thought he should be arrested. But they didn't
touch him. ⁴⁵ The Temple guard went back to the Pharisees and chief priests,
who asked, "Why didn't you arrest him?" ⁴⁶ "We never heard anyone speak like
him," said the guard. ⁴⁷ "Have you been fooled like the rest of them? ⁴⁸ Who
among us Pharisees, or any of your leaders believe in him? ⁴⁹ This rabble doesn't
know the Law—and they're damned for it." ⁵⁰ Nicodemus, a Pharisee who had
visited Jesus earlier, spoke up. ⁵¹ He asked, "Does the Law condemn someone
without hearing from that person? Mustn't we discover precisely what's been
done?" ⁵² "Are you from Galilee too?" they huffed. "Listen," they said, "nothing
mentions a prophet coming from Galilee." ⁵³ The meeting broke up and, one by
one, they went home.*

The mention here of living water will remind readers of Jesus' offer
of living water to the Samaritan woman [4:19]. Jesus' reference to
scripture—"from his depths springs living water"—is not a citation
of a specific verse. It's a succinct, personalized restatement of scripture's basic message that God has promised to sustain his children
always. Recall, for instance, God's production of water from rock
[Ex.17:6], and the vision of vast, life-giving waters in Ezekiel
[Ez.47:1–12]. Just as Jesus invited the woman at the well to believe
he was bringing God's promise to fulfillment, he invites the crowd
at the Feast of Tabernacles to believe he can satisfy their deepest
thirst—their thirst for divine life. John's comment that Jesus' scripture citation refers to the enlivening work of the Spirit will remind
readers of what they know will happen later: Jesus will show how
God's life is at work in us when he dies, is raised and is taken up to
glory; and when God's Spirit enters the world and enlivens all who
believe.

I assume John is deliberately creating a comic effect with his
description of the Pharisee's thick-headed smugness [vv.45–52]. But
if he leads us into laughter, he doesn't want to leave us there. After
all, why should we laugh? The Pharisees, in their various argu-
ments, are merely struggling to figure out how to respond to Jesus.
They're arguing over what would constitute a satisfactory proof,

assurance, or sign that Jesus should be believed. Are we not tempted to do the same? All of us—the Pharisees, the crowd, you, and I—tend to forget the sort of admonishment offered by the prophet Ezekiel: "The Lord asks, 'Whose way is just—yours, or mine?'" [Ez.18:25]. According to scripture, God's way of caring for his children can be explained only as an expression of divine love. To seek further explanations—to demand, "Why does God work the way he does; how, exactly, does he manage all of life; where are his blueprints?"—is to make oneself a judge of divine work. That makes no more sense than a typical airline passenger insisting in midflight that a pilot prove she can land the plane. Such a request, while laughably ridiculous, is also dangerously obtuse. If God cares for us precisely because we are his children, what good can come from trying—in our childlike state—to criticize his care? Nonetheless, that's what John describes the Pharisees and some in the crowd wanting to do. Jesus' invitation to let God quench their thirst—to bring them living water; to give them divine life—doesn't appeal to them. The scene ends with the sad detail of some of these unhappy people leaving for home alone.

EIGHT

Jesus, Still in Jerusalem, Is Heckled and Threatened

JESUS IS ASKED TO MAKE A JUDGMENT BASED ON THE LAW
[JN.8:1–11]

¹ [As that evening ended during the Feast of Tabernacles,] Jesus retired for the night to Mt. Olives. ² But he returned to the Temple early in the morning [as the feast continued]. All the people there came over to him, and, taking a seat, he began again to teach them. ³ But the scribes and Pharisees brought a woman to him who'd been caught in adultery. They stood her in the center of their delegation. ⁴ "Teacher," they said, "this woman was caught in the act of adultery. ⁵ The Law of Moses commands us to stone such a person. What say you?" ⁶ They wanted to entrap him in a violation of the Law. But Jesus leaned forward and doodled in the dust with his finger. ⁷ When they kept pestering him for an answer, he sat straight up and said, "The one who's without any sin should begin the stoning." ⁸ Then he leaned forward and doodled again on the ground. ⁹ This was their response: one by one they drifted away—the eldest first. As a result, the woman stood there alone. ¹⁰ Jesus sat up straight again and said, "My dear lady, where is everybody? Isn't there anyone to carry out your sentence?" ¹¹ She said, "No; no one." "Well," said Jesus, "I'm not going to pass judgment against you. Now, it's time for you to go—and sin no more."

—◦∅∅∅—

Let's look at this by first seeing how it ends. Jesus tells the woman to avoid sin—that is, to stop turning away from God [v.11]. He does this with the same abruptness with which he told the man he healed at the Sheep Pool to seek healing "from sinfulness" [5:15]. To Jesus, this advice is as fundamental and important as it is for a financial advisor to say, "Don't spend your money on get-rich-quick offers." Such basic advice may seem obvious. But, if it were, why would it need repeating? The fact is that, when we're driven by desire—for anything from sexual pleasure to vast wealth—the temptation to become self-obsessed or to abuse a trust can seem to overwhelm our ability to make the right choice. So Jesus tells the people he meets to develop a habit of making right choices. He asks them to notice at all times—not just at a time of temptation—how inclined they are to be selfish. In all his encounters, Jesus pushes past the white lies and equivocations that we use to pretend that, because we mean no harm, our choices are never too bad. He goes directly to the question we should always be asking ourselves: "What do you want?" If you don't want a life of free-floating confusion and anxiety, then stop trusting your pitiful notions of how things should work. Stop sinning. Turn, instead, to God. With all this in mind, we can appreciate how badly the scribes and Pharisees in this scene needed the advice Jesus gave the woman.

The authorities are described as petty and ridiculous in their attempt to entrap Jesus in wrongdoing. It's safe to assume that most readers will be appalled by the authorities' self-righteous show of defending the Law. Will readers imagine that, when the authorities finally walked away, each thought, "How foolishly I behaved!" Or do we suppose they were thinking, "Wait until next time"? If Jesus had said to them, "Go, and sin no more," do we suppose they'd have taken it to heart? If these questions seem easy to answer, that's because the lesson of the scene is so simple. Once again, Jesus has used something obvious—the Law—to teach about something obscure: the confusion in the human heart. To the authorities and to Jesus (and, one supposes, to the woman), it would have been clear that adultery was against the Law. But, to Jesus, something more was clear: people had forgotten the deeper purpose of the Law. The Law was not a measure of self-righteousness. It was a rich reminder that human activity is meant to spring from divine activity—that humans can do nothing without the power of God. Therefore, when we turn away from God, it is for our own good that we must turn back, and sin no more.

New Testament commentaries point out that this story is a late addition to the Gospel According to John. But readers of the Bible have read it as part of John's Gospel since the end of the fourth century, when it was included in the Vulgate translation of the Greek text into Latin. Its addition to the text raises scholarly questions about its source and about the motives of the editors who added it. These are intriguing questions. But Jesus' invitation to the woman to imagine a life completely dependent on God rather than on herself makes the scene a fitting part of the story that the evangelist has been unfolding—no matter when, how, or why later editors patched it into the narrative.

JESUS ONCE MORE DEFENDS HIS RIGHT TO TEACH
[JN.8:12–20]

[12] [After the encounter with the woman brought by the Pharisees,] Jesus spoke again. He said, "I am the light of the world. If you follow me, you will not drift in darkness. No, you'll have the light of life." [13] Some Pharisees said, "You speak for yourself. Your testimony can't be verified." [14] Jesus answered them, "Even if I am my own witness, it's a witness that can be verified. I know where I come from and where I'm going, but you don't know where I come from or where I'm going. [No, you don't know who I represent.] [15] You make judgments on others based only on your five senses. I don't make judgments for myself. [16] If, however, I did make a judgment, it would be accurate because I wouldn't base my judgment on my sense of things. I'd base it on the Father who sent me. [17] Even in the Law [of which you're so proud] it says the witness of two is reliable. [18] [So, first,] I testify for myself, and [second,] so does the Father who sent me." [19] They asked, "Where's your Father?" Jesus said, "You don't know me or the Father. If

you did know me, however, you'd know my Father too." [20] He taught openly, near the Temple treasury, but no attempt was made to arrest him. It wasn't his hour yet.

Here John describes Jesus making a stunning statement about being the world's light, which was greeted by a torrent of protest and much quibbling about authority. This intense, brief event should easily grab our attention. But, at this point, readers may have lost the narrative thread and become unsure who is listening as Jesus speaks. Earlier, John told us Jesus addressed the pilgrim crowd on "the last day of the feast" (see 7:37). In the scene just above, Jesus was described returning to the Temple "early in the morning" and being confronted by scribes and Pharisees [8:2–3]. Here, the narrative says Jesus "spoke to them again" [v.12] and that he did this "near the Temple treasury" [v.20].

First, if the timeline seems confusing, recall that "the last day of the feast" would have begun, like the Sabbath, in the evening. The following morning—when Jesus is described returning to the Temple and teaching in the area of the treasury—would have been the continuation of "the last day of the feast." As for the audience, it's natural to suppose that many pilgrims were packed into various areas of the Temple in the early morning of the climactic day of the feast, and that whatever crowd had gathered near the treasury listened to Jesus' words with interest—if only because he was responding forcefully to the cynical heckling of the authorities.

As John has described them, the authorities' obsession with silencing Jesus made them deaf to what they were hearing. Earlier, they'd been infuriated to hear the Temple guards repeat Jesus' promise to slake all thirst with living water [7:37–49]. In this scene, we hear the Pharisees trying to shut out Jesus' words about the light of life by claiming that Jesus had no right to teach without an authorized witness to back him up [v.13]. Although they don't say anything about the substance of Jesus' teaching, much less argue about its truth, it's hard to believe they didn't get his references to life-giving water and light. After all, everyone in Jerusalem had just spent several days celebrating a feast whose ceremonies of trust and thanksgiving centered on the use of water and light. Jesus apparently didn't think it was odd to teach about living water and divine light at such a feast. So we hear him inviting the Pharisees to notice how blind they were to the very thing they were supposedly celebrating: that God is always in their midst, and that they can always rejoice in his care.

We also hear Jesus say they could recognize his authority to teach simply by listening to his words. After all their study and reflection as religious authorities on God's promises to send prophets to remind his children of their Covenant, it seems incredible that these same authorities would have no idea where Jesus is from [v.14]. If they weren't so busy making judgments based exclusively on what their senses revealed to them, they'd be freer to notice how God makes judgments—and how Jesus relies on those judgments [vv.15–16]. It's amazing that they could have learned so little from scripture about the Father and the Father's ways [vv.17–19].

But the authorities seem to know only this: Jesus' teaching without their permission was an affront to the Law and a challenge to their power to interpret the Law. John describes Jesus attempting to help them see that their anxiety about their prerogatives blinds them to the truth. What's important is God's power, not theirs. And what God has decided to do with his power is to pour out gifts of divine nourishment, light, and life on all of us—and to give these gifts always. Although the Feast of Tabernacles celebrates the wonder and steadfastness of God's decision to love us, the Pharisees seem deaf to this truth as Jesus preaches it. According to John, everything the feast was meant to highlight was obscured by the Pharisees' lack of faith in God's judgment and their regard for their own judgments. Nonetheless, it wasn't the moment to stop teaching because, as John notes, Jesus' hour to finish his divine work hadn't come [v.20].

JESUS TEACHES THAT SIN—TURNING AWAY
FROM GOD—IS DEATH [JN.8:21–30]

[21] Jesus spoke up again [to the pilgrims and whoever else was in the Temple]. "I am going [to the one who sent me]. You'll keep wondering where I am [but you'll keep ignoring the obvious]. Yes, your sin [of self-obsession] will make you dead [to all but yourself]. So you can't come to where I'm going." [22] The people were baffled and wondered, "Is he talking about putting himself out of reach through suicide? Is that what he's going to do?" [23] Jesus said, "You're caught up in what's here below. I'm caught up in what's above. You're [mired] here in this world. I'm not. [24] It's as I just told you: your sins keep you dead. You'll remain dead in sinfulness if you don't believe I am [the one.]" [25] "Am the one what?" they asked. Jesus said, "Who I've always said I am. [26] I could say much in criticism of you. But [I'm not saying my personal opinion is true;] it's the one who sent me who is [speaking what's] true. Whatever truth I hear from him is the truth I tell the world." [27] They had no idea he was speaking of the Father. [28] So Jesus continued, "When you lift up the Son of Man, then you'll see that I am [the one sent by God]—that I do nothing by myself, and say only what I've been taught to say by the Father. [29] Because God sent me, he's with me. He never abandons me. He sees what I do and finds it good." [30] Many of those listening to the way Jesus spoke believed in him.

—◦◦◦—

Here we see Jesus offering his listeners the same simple choice that God, through Moses, offered in his description of the Covenant: "I have set before you life and death, the blessing and the curse. Choose life, then, that you and your descendants may live" [Dt.30:19]. The choice is so obvious that Jesus seems to think his listeners should be horrified to realize they'd made the wrong choice. But we hear that, no matter how he states and restates the same basic truth—that is, that he is sent from God, trusts God's promise of life, and therefore believes that he is heading for eternal life with God—his listeners continue to misunderstand him. For instance, though he's repeatedly said his only interest is the Father in heaven, his listeners suppose he's speaking of suicide when he talks of going away. Can that really be their best guess?

Is it also impossible for them to imagine what Jesus means when he says of himself, "I am" (see vv.24, 28)? Because his teaching has reaffirmed the Law, the prophets, and the Psalms, it has been consistent from the beginning. What you see Jesus doing and hear him saying represents exactly what the Father says and does. Anyone familiar with the scriptures should see that Jesus is consumed by the same concerns that occupy the God described in scripture. And yet, John depicts Jesus' fellow Jews as utterly lost when he says they should believe "I am." Rather than dismissing his words, they might have looked for an obvious meaning in them—such as "I am it"; "I am all there is"; "I am the one who speaks only God's word"; "I am bringing only God's light and life." They might even have recalled the story they would have heard since they were children: God told Moses from a burning bush that his name was "I am" (see Ex.3:13–14). Even readers who don't know much of the Old Testament will know that all the prophets tried (just as Jesus is again trying) to get the children of God to listen to God's truth. Readers may therefore be puzzled that so few of Jesus' listeners seemed to have learned the need for listening. Despite Jesus' talk about going where there is *no sin*; about being caught up with what's *above*; about speaking only the truth of the *one who sent* him, his listeners haven't gathered that he's speaking about the Father [v.27].

Finally, after Jesus assures them that they'll understand his simple statement, "I am," when they lift him up and discover the truth that God is always with us and never abandons us, we're told that many believed in him. What do we suppose that means? Did they understand that, when Jesus called himself "I am," he was saying, "I am the one who brings healing—like the lifted-up serpent in the wilderness" [Num.21:6–9; see above, 3:14]? Did they think Jesus used the expression "I am" to mean, "I am the one who has no doubt that God is with me and will never leave me"? In other words: were they finding Jesus' confidence and trust in the Father attractive, and might they have hoped to experience that same trust and confidence—were they coming to believe in God just as Jesus believed in him?

DISCIPLESHIP DESCRIBED AS A STRUGGLE WITH SIN
[JN.8:30–43]

[30] Many of those in the Temple listening to Jesus believed in him. [31] He said to those who believed: "You'll be true, willing disciples if you keep listening to me. [32] [And, if you listen,] you'll know what's true—a truth that will free you." [33] They said. "We're the children of Abraham. We've never been slaves. Why do you talk about freeing us?" [34] "O, yes; O, yes. O, yes indeed, I'm saying that you're not truly free unless you're freed from sin. [35] [Everyone knows that] slaves, though part of a household, are not part of the family, but children are always part of the family. [36] (Of course, a slave can be given freedom by the heir of the house.) [37] I understand your claim to be children of Abraham. But, you [children of Abraham] are trying to kill me. Why? Because my words don't touch your hearts! [38] I've been teaching you what the Father and I see. You should hear [the words that come from] the Father. And you should act on what you hear." [39] They said, "Father? Our father is Abraham." Jesus said, "If you were children of Abraham, you'd behave like him. [40] But, instead, you plot to kill me—a man who speaks the truth heard from God. That wasn't Abraham's reaction to the truth. [41] O, yes, you behave just like your father, indeed!" They said, "Are you calling us bastards? We have a father—God!" [42] Jesus said, "If God were your Father, you would have loved me because I came from him. I didn't send myself. I was sent by him. [43] Why don't you understand me? Why? Because you won't even begin to listen to me!"

John doesn't say how some of the Jews in the Temple manifested a belief in Jesus. He simply says some believed, and that Jesus called them to experience the freedom of fully understanding truth [vv.30–32]. The exchange quickly becomes confused, as the "believers" take Jesus' call to freedom as an insult to their status [v.33]. Jesus then insists that true freedom is freedom from sin—from all that separates us from God [v.34]. He compares this freedom to the way the status of household slaves can be changed from family servants to family members: the rightful heir can give them the new status [vv.35–36]. Expanding on this image of family status, Jesus says true heirs of Abraham wouldn't close their hearts to his words. He even equates rejection of his words with the opposition of the authorities who want to kill him [v.37; cf. 7:14–25]. Depicting himself as the Father's rightful heir (i.e., as one who completely accepts his relationship with the Father), he says his listeners should emulate his words and actions (i.e., accept the gift of the status God wants to give them) [v.38]. The so-called believers ignore this invitation to reflect on their need for a closer relationship with God. Instead, they tout their closeness to Abraham—an assertion Jesus challenges [vv.39–41a]. The listeners deflect this challenge by suddenly boasting about their status as children of God [v.41b]. Jesus then tells them that, if they were children of God, they would recognize him as their sibling, and they would listen to him. But their exalted assumptions about themselves keep them from accepting Jesus' teaching that a true disciple always needs to learn more about God [vv.42–43].

This scene (which continues below) depicts the belligerence of some new disciples in reaction to Jesus' words—belligerence strong enough, it seems, for the teacher to interpret it as a wish to murder him! If this strikes a reader as extraordinary, it might be helpful to recall that, from the beginning of John's Gospel (see Nathanael's first reaction to Jesus [1:46]), Jesus has encountered people who have rigid assumptions about God—assumptions Jesus never hesitates to challenge. According to John, Jesus repeatedly encouraged his listeners to realize that to believe in God means to be part of an unfolding relationship—a relationship in which each believer's trust will face many struggles and doubts. Jesus therefore tells his disciples that, if they want their relationship with God to grow to fullness, they will have to keep listening and learning.

As a reader tries to picture Jesus' audience in this scene, it may help to keep in mind that Jesus is addressing people in the Temple on the last day of a great feast. Imagine the pilgrims coming and going; stopping for a while to listen; drifting away again; talking to one another and making jokes or comments; and—as we see in this exchange—arguing with the teacher. Imagine, too, Jesus' reaction to this shifting audience and to the fact that some faces look interested, some puzzled, and some downright menacing. Notice that, throughout all this, Jesus continues to invite his listeners to open up their hearts to his word—to turn away from their burdensome assumptions, and turn to God's Good News.

JESUS TEACHES ABOUT WICKEDNESS; THE CROWD REJECTS HIS TEACHING [JN.8:44–59]

44 [Jesus continued to confront the people in the Temple about their unwillingness to listen.] He said, "Your father is the devil [not God]. You do what he wants. [And look how he behaves!] He always takes life; he never speaks the truth; nothing true is in him; lying is his only language. He is a liar—the father of lies.
45 [Because the father of lies is your father,] when I speak the truth, of course you don't believe me. 46 Who here can reproach me for sin? Well, then, if I'm telling the truth, why don't you believe me? 47 If you belonged to God, you'd hear God's word. The reason you don't listen to God's word is that you don't belong to him."
48 The crowd responded to this with, "Tell us we're not right to call you a Samaritan [a dabbler with devils] and possessed as well!" 49 Jesus responded, "I'm not possessed by a demon. I give honor only to my Father—and you don't respect me for that at all. 50 I'm not looking to glorify myself. But there is someone who has decided to glorify me—the one who judges rightly and makes right decisions. 51 O, yes; O, yes. O yes, indeed, I'm telling you that those who take in my word are taking in freedom from death—they'll never know death."
52 The crowd said, "Now it's obvious you're possessed by a demon! [How do we know?] Abraham died. The prophets died. But you're saying, 'Whoever takes in my word will not die.' 53 Do you think you're more important than our father, Abraham—who died! More important than the prophets—who died! Just who do you think you are?" 54 Jesus told them, "If I glorify myself, that's meaningless. But my Father is the one who gives me glory. Yes, the one you say is your God! 55 You don't know the Father. I do. If I acted like you—as though I didn't know him—I'd be a liar. But, because I know the Father, I take in his word. 56 Abraham, who you insist is your father, was happy to see my day. Yes, he saw my

day and was delighted." [57] The crowd said, "Wait! You're not even fifty, but you've seen Abraham?" [58] Jesus said, "O, yes; O, yes. O yes, indeed, I say that before Abraham was, I am." [There it was again, that infuriating "I am."] [59] So they gathered stones to throw. But Jesus hid, and then left the Temple.

—◦◦◦—

Here, the argument begun in the last section continues. John describes Jesus going directly to the root of his audience's inability to listen. He says they've made themselves children of the devil: "Like your father, the devil, you tell yourselves lies—and believe them! When someone restates the simple truth, you can't accept it" [v.46]. How insulting this must sound to those who consider themselves children of God. But Jesus isn't insulting his audience. He's pleading with them to see the seriousness of their situation. If they belonged to God, if they actually lived as God's children, they would, of course, always hear him speaking to them. It isn't foolish to expect God to speak to you. Parents are always talking to their children. If this crowd doesn't hear God speaking to them, it means they are no longer God's children.

As John continues the scene, Jesus' audience responds to his description of them by claiming he is insane. Jesus carefully points out that his words are not irrational. He speaks only about God, their Father. He's never said or done anything to suggest he's promoting some mad endeavor. He wants only to do the Father's work [v.49]. His audience knows from scripture that the work God most ardently wants to accomplish is to make them his children—to share his life with them forever. Because of God's decision to share his glory, Jesus says he has no need to seek glory for himself [v.50]. His words repeat what the crowd should already know. They too are meant to share divine life and glory—to live forever [v.51]. But the crowd responds to this reminder of God's intentions with another accusation of madness. They know that everyone dies. Does Jesus not know, for instance, that Abraham and all the prophets are dead?

That might seem like a good place for Jesus to end the argument. As John describes them, the people in the crowd weren't willing to consider anything but their own point of view—which, in this case, was limited to what they knew about life [vv.52–53]. But John tells us Jesus didn't let them pretend there was nothing more to life than what they saw of it. He pictures Jesus again saying he refused to exalt his own will; instead, he trusted God's promise of divine glory—divine life. Unlike them, Jesus wanted to take in God's word [vv.54–55].

When we hear Jesus say that Abraham was able to foresee this day [v.56]—that is, a day when someone takes in the whole word of God—we again hear the crowd sticking with their crabbed view of life. Their retort that Jesus was too young to have seen Abraham [v.57] contains an implicit question they could have addressed and answered for themselves. A possible response to their unspoken question (i.e., "How could Abraham have seen Jesus' day?") is that Abraham chose to trust God by imagining God's word was true, and that his promises would be fulfilled. But because the crowd didn't answer this question for themselves, Jesus answered it for them. And his answer shocked them: "Before Abraham was, I am" [v.58]. John describes this bare statement hitting them with more force than Jesus' earlier statement, "I am" [8:24]. Here, Jesus' response seems too close to the response Moses received when he asked God how he should speak of him to the Israelites—when God answered, "Say I AM sent you" [Ex.3:14]. The crowd's only thought was that Jesus was brazenly making himself God. They therefore felt it was their duty to execute him for blasphemy by stoning him to death. This was their expression of resistance to everything Jesus said.

Throughout John's description of this teaching session, the crowd failed repeatedly to accept that Jesus might be speaking the truth—despite his constant appeals to what they'd heard from scripture. The crowd refused to consider the possibility that Jesus was speaking the truth even when, building on their own claim to be proud descendants of Abraham [8:33], he invited them to imitate Abraham's trust. If they were truly in awe of the faith of Abraham;

if they were deeply convinced that God, who promised to care for them, would send another great prophet like Moses [Dt.18:15]; if, in other words, their hearts were in some small part moved as Jesus' heart was moved by God's assurances of a loving union, they might have been willing to think—at least for a moment—about Jesus' words, "I am." Their thoughts might have run like this: "Abraham trusted God. He believed God was at work in the world around him. He also learned to believe that God was at work inside him. The reason Abraham let God direct his life seemed obvious to him: God was God and he, Abraham, was not. He let God shape his life—his very being—despite the fact that he couldn't comprehend how God was bringing about this intimate union." But the crowd didn't allow themselves a similar train of thought. Up to this point in the Gospel, Jesus' experiences have confirmed as true what he'd heard from scripture: God gives divine glory to all who ask for it. Jesus knew that his heart was hungry for nothing but this divine glory. He embodied the truth that God is pouring himself out—and has done so "from the beginning" [1:1]. Jesus can say, "I am that truth. I am what you see: God giving glory to us. I am the presence of God." Jesus wanted people to imagine the possibility that they could say the same thing. But they wouldn't listen.

NINE

Jesus Teaches by Healing a Blind Man

JESUS AND HIS DISCIPLES ENCOUNTER A BLIND MAN
[JN.9:1–12]

[1] *As Jesus walked along, he saw a man who'd been born blind.* [2] *His disciples asked, "Teacher, what's your opinion; was this man born blind because of his parents' sins or his own?"* [3] *Jesus said, "[As for his being born blind,] it wasn't to punish either him or the parents for sin. It was to reveal in him God's glorious working.* [4] *Because I'm sent by God, let's do his [glorious] works while we have the day. The night falls fast, when no one can work.* [5] *But, for the time being, the world has light because I'm in it."* [6] *He then spat on the ground and made mud with his spit. He dabbed the mud on the blind man's eyes.* [7] *And he told him, "Go wash in the pool called Siloam." This name was commonly interpreted to mean, "Someone Is Sent." So, the man went, washed, and came away seeing.* [8] *The man's neighbors and others who'd known him as a beggar said, "This can't be the man who used to beg!"* [9] *Some said, "Yes!" Others said, "No, it's someone who looks like him." But the man said, "It's me."* [10] *"But how were your eyes opened?" people asked.* [11] *He said, "That one, the one called Jesus, made mud, put it on my eyes, and told me, 'Go to the Pool of Sending and wash.' So, I went to the pool, I washed, and I saw."* [12] *"Where is this fellow?" they asked. He said, "I don't know."*

——✿✿✿——

The abrupt change of scene might provoke the film producer in us again—see comments on 6:16–21. "Wait," we say. "How does this follow from the last scene? What happened to the crowd in the Temple who wanted to stone Jesus? From where did his disciples suddenly appear?" John leaves us to imagine that the disciples may have been with Jesus all along—lurking, perhaps, on the sidelines during the argument in the Temple; slipping out sheepishly behind him when he left [8:59b]. John also lets us guess how the crowd abandoned their pursuit of Jesus. (Perhaps they found solace in sharing their high dudgeon among themselves.) What John does describe is Jesus moving on from the uproar in the Temple and sometime later (perhaps just outside Jerusalem) continuing to teach the truth he's taught all along: God's glory is revealed in us.

This scene starts with a simple lesson for the disciples. It builds on lessons previously taught. At Cana, the disciples saw God's glory when Jesus was moved by his mother's faith that God was at work in the young couple's need [2:11]. It's reasonable to suppose the disciples were also witnesses to Jesus' response to the faith of the royal official [4:54]; and that they were with Jesus in Jerusalem when he defended his cure of the sick man at the Sheep Pool by saying that, as long as the Father is at work, he would be at work [5:17]. They were there on the mountain when Jesus gave thanks to the Father and fed thousands [6:11]. And they heard his command not to be afraid when he came to them on the sea [6:20]. Each of these events is a lesson in putting one's faith in God. And the reason for placing trust in God is the same reason suggested in the first creation story: "God made humans in his own image" [Gen.1:27]— that is, God loves us as he loves himself. For those who believe in this loving God, there can be no doubt whose care we should choose when we're in need of comfort, consolation, nourishment, healing, and peace. This is the God Jesus believes in—the God whose glory he invites the disciples to see in the healing of a blind man.

But, as John tells the story, the disciples weren't the only witnesses of the blind man's cure. We're told that, when neighbors and acquaintances of the man born blind noticed he could see, they didn't notice or praise God's glory. Instead, they began an inquisition.

INTERROGATION OF THE MAN WHO HAD BEEN BORN BLIND [JN.9:13–23]

¹³ Some [in the crowd of doubters] took the man who had been blind to the Pharisees. ¹⁴ (By the way, Jesus made mud and opened the man's eyes on a Sabbath.) ¹⁵ The Pharisees asked him how he gained his sight. He told them, "He put mud on my eyes. I washed. I see." ¹⁶ Some of the Pharisees said, "That man's not from God. He doesn't keep the Sabbath!" But other Pharisees said, "How could a sinful man accomplish such signs?" Their opinions divided them. ¹⁷ So they turned back to the blind man and asked, "What's your opinion of him? After all, he opened your eyes." He said, "He's a prophet." ¹⁸ They couldn't believe he'd gained his sight after being born blind. So they called for the parents of this newly seeing man. ¹⁹ "Is this your son?" they asked. "Do you attest that he was born blind? [If so,] how do you explain that he can see?" ²⁰ The parents said, "We know this is our son. We know he was born blind. ²¹ But we don't know how he can see; and we don't know who could have opened his eyes. Question him. He's old enough. He'll speak for himself." ²² His parents spoke this way because they were afraid of the Jewish authorities. The authorities had decided that anyone who said Jesus was the Messiah—the Anointed One of God—would be cut off from the synagogue. ²³ That was the reason the parents said, "He's old enough. Question him."

—◦◦◦—

John could presume that readers would remember what they learned earlier: if Jesus heals on a Sabbath, he'll face accusations of breaking the Law (see 5:9–18). Here, as before, the Pharisees' rush to judgment is almost comical. But their inquiry turns into a farce when witnesses won't give them the answers they want. Their huffy self-assurance may remind us of other facetious comments made about Jesus' words and works—think, for example, of Nathanael, and of the woman at the well. Here, despite the difference of opinion among the Pharisees [v.16], the faction that is in favor of unmasking sinners is so blindly driven by their prejudice that they attempt to prove two conflicting facts: one, someone broke the Sabbath by healing and, two, no healing occurred. They grill the newly seeing man about healing [v.17] but doubt he was ever blind [v.18], so they haul in the parents for questioning [vv.19–21].

Scholars tell us the comment about Jews being officially forbidden to speak of Jesus as Messiah [v.22] may have been added by a subsequent editor to reflect a later regulation within the Jewish community. But, as it stands, the verse reminds readers that an air of suspicion and menace had begun to encircle Jesus. Recall the rumors at the Feast of Tabernacles (7:12–13).

THE INTERROGATION CONTINUES [JN.9:24–34]

[24] They called again upon the man who'd been born blind. "Give glory only to God," they said. "We know this man's a sinner." [25] The man said, "I don't know if he's a sinner. But I do know this: I was blind. Now I see." [26] They asked, "What did he do to you? How did he open your eyes?" [27] "I told you already," he said. "You didn't listen. Do you want another hearing because you'd like to be his disciples?" [28] They sneered and said, "You're that man's disciple! We, on the other hand, are disciples of Moses. [29] We know God spoke to Moses. We have no idea where this man comes from." [30] The man said, "That's amazing: you can't imagine where he comes from even though you know he opened my eyes! [31] We know God doesn't listen to [the ravings of] sinners. But God does listen to someone who reveres him and does his will. [32] It's never been heard of that someone opened the eyes of a man born blind. [33] If this man were not from God, he couldn't have done such a thing." [34] They said, "You [were born with the curse of blindness and thus] were born a complete sinner. You would teach us?" Then they threw him out of their midst.

—⌘—

John gives us a blast of irony in the first words of the Pharisees' second investigation: "Give glory only to God" [v.24]. That's what Jesus and the healed man are doing; but the Pharisees think they know that can't be so. In fact, they're sure the opposite is true; Jesus is a sinner. Their obstinate blindness to the truth is a stunning contrast to the willing embrace of it by the newly seeing man. And the man's challenge to their benighted opinion makes for amusing reading. How can these learned authorities get things so wrong? Beneath all the touches of humor, however, there's a dismaying fact. These men are so desperate to get at the truth, and so sure of their ability to find it, they can't seem to hear anything but their own overheated words. They cannot let themselves rejoice in the man's healing any more than they can listen to his simple logic. They are, as they themselves say, unteachable [v.34].

JESUS ASKS THE NEWLY SEEING MAN IF HE BELIEVES
[JN.9:35–41]

35 When Jesus heard that the Pharisees had cast the man out, he looked for him. He asked him, "Do you believe in the Son of Man?" 36 "For me to believe in him," he said, "I have to know who he is." 37 "You've seen him," said Jesus. "He's speaking with you." 38 "I do believe," he said. And he bent down in worship. 39 Jesus said, "I've come into the world to make a judgment—to speak the truth. I reveal this truth so that those who don't see might see. As for those who [say they] see, the truth should reveal their blindness." 40 Some Pharisees nearby heard Jesus' words and said, "You don't mean to say we are blind, do you?" 41 Jesus said, "If you were blind [i.e., if there was no way for you to see the truth], there would be no sin in that. But you insist that you see [i.e., that you already know the truth]. That's your sin."

—⟞ᴼᴼ⟝—

John told us Jesus asked the man healed at the Sheep Pool to reflect on spiritual health [5:14]. Here he tells us Jesus asked another person whose body he'd healed to reflect on spiritual healing. In this case, he wants to know if the man who was born blind is willing to believe in "the Son of Man" [v.35]. The man confesses his ignorance, but says he's ready to learn [v.36]—a reaction similar to the reaction of the woman at the well (see 4:24–26). Like her, this man seems ready to believe God's promise to send to his children a specially chosen one—an Anointed One, a Messiah. When Jesus says he's the one whom God has sent, the man confesses his belief and he thanks Jesus for moving him to this confession.

It seems so simple and easy for the newly seeing man. Unlike the Pharisees, he doesn't launch a full investigation of how God could accomplish his will through the work of a wandering nobody like Jesus. Instead, after reviewing the facts—with the bullying help of the Pharisees—he doesn't pretend to see how they fit together. All he knows is that Jesus put mud on his eyes, told him to wash them, and they opened [9:15].

Jesus' judgment is that the man is right to recognize this deeper blindness. Because of it, he must seek another source of enlightenment. So, he accepts as true Jesus' assurance that God's chosen one speaks to him [v.37]. He believes that Jesus—this particular Son of Man, who puts all his trust in God—brings divine light. The Pharisees, sadly, feel no need for the divine light Jesus brings. They insist they can see by their own light. How dreadful to be so bedazzled.

TEN

Jesus Asks His Listeners Whom They Want to Follow; Another Feast

EVEN SHEEP KNOW WHOM TO FOLLOW [JN.10:1–10]

[1] "O, yes; O, yes. O yes, indeed, I say this to you: anyone who doesn't use the gate to go into a sheep pen, but climbs over the fence, is a thief—a rustler. [2] The one who uses that gate to go into the pen is the shepherd of the sheep. [3] The gatekeeper is there to open up for him. The sheep hear his voice and recognize their names as he calls them. He can lead them out. [4] When he's gotten all the sheep that belong to him out of the pen, he goes on ahead of them. They follow him because his voice is familiar to them. [5] But they won't follow a stranger. They run away from strangers because their voices are unfamiliar." [6] Jesus offered them this image, but they had no idea what he was talking about. [7] So Jesus continued his lesson: "O, yes; O, yes. O yes, indeed, this is what I'm saying: I'm the gate for the sheep. [8] The others who came were thieves and rustlers. The sheep didn't listen to them. [9] I'm the gate. Those who go through me will be safe. They'll come in. They'll go out. They'll find pasture. [10] A thief comes to rob, kill, and butcher. I came so that they could have life—life in its fullness."

Notice that, although there was an attempt on Jesus' life in the Temple at the end of the Feast of Tabernacles [8:59], John hasn't said that Jesus traveled away from Jerusalem or out of Judea. John has described Jesus' departures from Jerusalem several times before (see 1:43; 3:22; 4:3; 6:1). The absence of any mention of one here suggests that the reader should picture Jesus moving about and teaching near Jerusalem sometime after the Feast of Tabernacles. We might even imagine that Jesus is still addressing the same group of Pharisees who, in the last scene, couldn't imagine their need for enlightenment; or Jesus may have moved on.

The obvious simplicity of Jesus' picture of sheep following a familiar shepherd doesn't need a special setting or audience. Anyone who's ever stopped on a trip through the country to let their kids feed some sheep grazing in a pasture will know how quickly sheep bolt from a stranger. If the disappointed kids linger long enough to see the farmer enter the pasture, they'll see how eagerly the flock runs toward a dependable source of food. Jesus wants his listeners to ask themselves, "Where do you look for care? Do you see yourself running to anyone who waves a handful of weeds over the fence? Does anyone come to mind when you worry, 'Who will care for me in my need?'" Implicit in Jesus' picture of shepherd and sheep is another question: "Do you see yourself as needy?"

John tells us that, when Jesus' listeners didn't understand his first image, he patiently offered another image. Picture this, he says: "Suppose I'm the gate for a sheep pen. How would you describe those who wanted to avoid this gate—who tried to get at the sheep some other way? Yes, they'd be thieves! Would the sheep listen to these interlopers? No" [vv.7–8].

Or, he says, picture this: "If you imagine me as the gate, you see sheep entering the safety of the pen through me; and you see them going out through me to safe pasture. But, if you picture a thief slipping into the pen, you see slaughter. So, ask yourselves, why have I come? I've come to bring the fullness of life" [vv.9–10].

If readers have supposed that Jesus is still addressing the Pharisees who assumed they were enlightened [9:40–41], it's easy to guess that they would take offense at Jesus' implications. But Jesus' point is the same no matter who is listening. And, as far as the evangelist is concerned, Jesus' words are also being addressed to us. We're being asked to consider whether we assume we're able to get ourselves out of all dangers and away from all threats. We're being challenged to ponder whether we hope merely for lives of moderate safety and contentment, or whether we desire to become so fully alive that we are freed from all fear of death. Put simply, do we believe that Jesus is bringing us to life in its divine fullness?

JESUS DESCRIBES HIMSELF AS THE PERFECT SHEPHERD
[JN.10:11–21]

[11] "I am the perfect shepherd," said Jesus. "I give my life for my sheep. [12] A hired hand, who's not the shepherd, will run away, leaving the sheep if a wolf attacks. The wolf brings sheep down and scatters the flock. [13] The hired hand behaves like this because the tending is done for pay, not out of concern for the sheep. [14] I'm a perfect shepherd. I know my sheep. My sheep know me. [15] It's the same way my Father knows me and I know the Father. So [of course] I give my life for my sheep. [16] And there are other sheep not in this flock. I'll gather them together too. They'll listen to my voice. All will become one flock. There will be one shepherd. [17] This is why the Father loves me: I give my life so that I can take it up again. [18] No one can take my life from me. I give it willingly. I can give my life; I can take it up again. That's what my Father asks me to do." [19] Because of these words, there was another disagreement among his listeners. [20] Many said, "He's got demons. He's crazy. There's no point listening to him." [21] Others said, "These words aren't like those of a possessed person. Can a demon open the eyes of a blind man?"

—⟨ɷɷɷ⟩—

In the image that preceded this description, Jesus was asking what our hopes were in life. Here he tells us what they should be. We should want and expect a perfect shepherd—one that knows all our needs and will never abandon us [vv.11–14]. (Does that sound familiar? If not, see Ex.6:7–8.) John doesn't want us to miss Jesus' point here, so he has him say something astonishing in order to emphasize it. The intimate relationship of care and concern that Jesus imagines he has with us is the same intimate relationship that the Father has with him. Just as God is always pouring out and giving himself to the Word [1:1–2], Jesus will pour himself out for us [v.15].

John tells us Jesus extended the image of his role as shepherd of a flock to reveal how he was determined to share his life with all those who hear his word [v.16]. He then describes Jesus explaining why he was so confident he could lead his sheep to the fullness of life: he believed the Father was giving him divine life. So he didn't need to hold on to life. He could let it go, trusting that the Father, who never stops sharing life with him, would let him take it up again. It shouldn't surprise us to read that the Father loves Jesus for his act of trust in him. Jesus' desires and the Father's are in perfect accord [vv.17–18].

We hear that some of Jesus' listeners regarded his words as the ravings of a madman. Others were attracted to what he had to say — especially when they recalled how Jesus touched peoples' lives with healing [vv.20–21].

JESUS, IN JERUSALEM FOR ANOTHER FEAST, OFFERS DIVINE LIFE [JN.10:22–30]

22 It was now winter—the time of the Feast of the Dedication of the Temple in Jerusalem. [This was when it was recalled that, over one hundred and fifty years earlier, the Temple had been consecrated anew after a Syrian invasion. It was a time for people to renew their commitment to the Lord.] 23 Jesus was strolling in the outer court of the Temple, along the colonnade called Solomon's Portico. 24 Jewish pilgrims surrounded him and asked, "Why are you making us hold our breath? If you're God's Anointed One, tell us." 25 "I've told you," Jesus said. "But you don't believe. Look at the works I do in my Father's name. That should tell you what you want to know. 26 But you don't know and you don't believe because you're not my sheep. 27 My sheep hear me. I know them. They follow me. 28 I give them eternal life. They will not die—ever. No one can snatch them out of my care. [29] My Father has given them to me. He's greater than all. No one takes them away from the Father's care. [30] I and the Father are one."

———∽∘∕∘∽———

When we're told that Jesus strolled about the Temple just a few months after the life-threatening climax of his last visit (see 8:59), we may wonder whether he's acting carelessly or confidently. John quickly makes it clear that it's Jesus' confident commitment to his mission that draws him back to the Temple at a time when it will be crowded for a feast. Interrupted in his peaceful stroll, Jesus has a swift response to the complaints of his fellow Jews that he is being evasive. He tells them he hasn't been secretive or mysterious. He has repeatedly explained that his words and actions are directed by his Father—their Father. He tells them they are ignorant about his mission because they refuse to open up to the possibility that his words and actions might help them. They refuse to be cared for—they don't want to be his sheep [vv.25–26].

But we hear Jesus tell them that those who do choose to listen to him, follow him, and allow him to care for them will find themselves living eternal life [vv.27–28]. John then describes Jesus explaining that eternal life is a gift from his Father. (This is the gift the Father spelled out and promised in the Covenant—a Covenant he has repeatedly renewed.) Jesus has the same trust in the blessings of the Covenant that the Father has; in this, he and the Father are one [vv.29–30].

JESUS' OFFER OF DIVINE LIFE IS REJECTED [JN.10:31–42]

[31] As the Temple crowd had done once before, they picked up stones to stone Jesus. [32] He said, "You've seen me do many of my Father's works—work that he finds very good. Which are you stoning me for?" [33] They said, "We're not stoning you for good works, but for blasphemy. You're a man, but you say you're God!" [34] Jesus said, "Doesn't scripture say, 'You are gods, children of the Most High— yes, all of you' [Ps.82:6]? [35] They're addressed as gods. You can't unsay what scripture says. [36] So if the Father consecrates me and sends me into the world,

how can I blaspheme by saying, 'I am the Son of God'? *³⁷ If I don't do my Father's work, don't believe me. ³⁸ But if I do his works, believe the works—even if you don't believe me. If you do believe, you'll realize that the Father is in me, and I am in the Father." ³⁹ Once again, they tried to arrest him. But he slipped away from them. ⁴⁰ He went back across the Jordan, where John had first baptized. He stayed there. ⁴¹ Many came to him. They were saying to one another, "Though John didn't accomplish signs, all the things he said about this man were true." ⁴² Many who had come to him believed in him.*

The text says "the Jews" picked up stones [v.31], and "the Jews" answered Jesus [v.33]. But, as we've seen before, "Jews" can't mean all Jews—or, in this instance, all the Jews gathered for the Feast of the Dedication. John has described Jews who are impressed by Jesus' words (see 7:40; 9:18). But here "the Jews" are individuals who, like the authorities blinded by their punctilious interpretation of the Law, refused to mull over what Jesus was saying.

We hear Jesus asking them to notice the disparity between what they thought and what they saw. They saw Jesus do things that reflected God's care and revealed God's glory, yet they thought he was wrong to speak about the intimate connection between himself and God [v.32]. According to John, Jesus failed to move them. As far as they were concerned, doing God's will and work didn't unite you with God [v.33]. Then we hear Jesus refer them to scripture, asking why, if God calls all his children gods, he, as God's Son, couldn't behave and act like God [vv.34–36]. Take another look, says Jesus (ever the patient teacher). He asks them to notice that he doesn't claim to work for himself, but for the Father. If the works he's been moved to do for those in need remind them of God's promise of everlasting care, perhaps they might consider the possibility that God is truly at work in him. And if he and the Father are dedicated to the same work, why shouldn't he speak of himself and the Father as united—as one [vv.37–38]? Then John describes Jesus once more failing to persuade them to listen to this possibility. In fact, they would like to stop his talking altogether. But, says John, he slipped away [v.39].

Jesus' retreat from Judea to the other side of the Jordan [v.40] may remind readers of his first departure from Jerusalem [3:22] after the mixed reaction to his "signs" and his eviction of merchants from the Temple. But between then and now, resistance to his words has evolved past irritated questions from the authorities (see 2:18, 20) and the mild condescension of Nicodemus [3:4]. Once again some people find Jesus' words so inconceivable and shocking that they feel he must be silenced with a sentence of death (see 8:59).

Although John describes this teaching encounter in the Temple as another example of Jesus failing to touch the hearts of many pilgrims gathered in Jerusalem for a feast, he doesn't conclude this part of his narrative by emphasizing defeat or danger. Instead, he mentions that some people did listen to Jesus—and learned something. They noticed that John the Baptist's words about Jesus had turned out to be true: Jesus was indeed someone who was rightly called the Lamb of God [1:29–34] since he did nothing but the works of God, his Father. So, apparently, they continued to listen to Jesus; and they began to believe him [vv.41–42]. Their positive reaction to Jesus' teaching isn't described as a complete transformation of their hearts. They were not suddenly overwhelmed by the Spirit. But John has made the point that, for those prepared to listen to Jesus' words, it's possible to experience what it's like to believe. In other words, careful listening and reflection can help you choose to believe.

ELEVEN

Jesus Calls Lazarus to Life; the Authorities Plot Jesus' Death

JESUS' DISCIPLES ARE PUZZLED BY HIS REACTION TO
LAZARUS'S ILLNESS [JN.11:1–16]

¹ [Some months passed.] There was a man who'd fallen sick, Lazarus, who lived with his sisters, Mary and Martha, in the village of Bethany. ² [As we'll see later in the story,] Mary is the one who rubs Jesus' feet with ointment and dries them with her hair. It was her brother, Lazarus, who was sick. ³ The sisters sent news to Jesus, telling him, "Lord, your friend is sick." ⁴ But when Jesus got the news, he said, "His sickness is not to result in death, but in the glory of God. And because of that, the Son of God will be glorified." ⁵ Jesus truly loved Martha, her sister, and Lazarus. ⁶ But, despite hearing the news of the sickness, Jesus stayed for two days where he was [i.e., the other side of the Jordan, where he'd moved earlier; see 10:40]. ⁷ Then he said to his disciples, "Let's go back to Judea." ⁸ "Teacher," they said, "not long ago the Jews there were trying to stone you. You want to go back?" ⁹ He said, "Are there twelve hours of daylight? If you walk about in daylight, you don't stumble. You can see by the light of this world. ¹⁰ But if you walk at night, you stumble because you don't have a light in you." ¹¹ A while after he'd said this, he told them, "Our friend Lazarus has fallen asleep. I'm going to awaken him." ¹² "Lord," they said, "if he's able to sleep, he'll get well." ¹³ Jesus was talking about death. The disciples thought he meant the sleep of healing. [14] So Jesus said plainly, "Lazarus died. [15] For your sake, I'm glad I wasn't there. Now you may believe. We'll go to him." [16] Thomas—called Didymus, "the Twin"—said, "We'll go so we may die with him."

—◦◦◦—

It's hard not to suppose that Jesus' disciples felt dispirited after their last hasty retreat with him from Jerusalem. What did they think they would do as they kept away from Judean territory on the other side of the Jordan—start baptizing again? No matter what their thoughts may have been, they were interrupted by sad news: Jesus' friend, Lazarus, was sick [vv.1–3]. Now what? As John has described him, Jesus doesn't see sickness, worry, anxiety, or pressing needs as other people do. (Recall his initial responses to the two incidents at Cana—see 2:4; 4:48.) All human experience, as far as he's concerned, is shot through with the glory of God. That's what he looks for, and invites others to see [v.4].

Because readers are alerted to the fact that Jesus sees Lazarus's sickness as an opportunity to reveal God's glory [v.4], they won't necessarily be surprised that he waits two days before making a move. Nor should they be surprised that, after the two-day delay, Jesus decides to travel to Bethany. The disciples, on the other hand, fear the village's proximity to Jerusalem and the Jerusalem authorities [vv.5–8]. But all can agree—both the disciples and all of us—that Jesus offers commonsense advice when he says we should walk about only when there's enough light to see where we're going [vv.9–10].

However, we don't always follow commonsense advice. Jesus' remark that none of us has light "in us" [v.10] reminds us that all light comes from without. We're not our own sources of light—or enlightenment. Nonetheless, we repeatedly assume we understand things that we don't actually comprehend or even see. We push ahead with ready answers even though we're operating in the dark—in ignorance. The disciples do this in their response to Jesus' plan to go and wake Lazarus [v.11]. They presume that Lazarus's sleeping indicates the passing of his crisis; he must now be resting comfortably. They're content with their analysis of Lazarus's condition and with their implied opinion that nothing more need be done [vv.12–13]. They consider no other possibilities—despite the fact that Jesus has said that he wants to go back to Judea [v.7] to reveal God's glory in this crisis [v.4]. Jesus tries to refocus their thinking by spelling out the facts as he sees them: Lazarus is dead; this situation might help them believe; they're all going to Bethany [vv.14–15].

Despite the clarity of these simple statements from Jesus, the scene ends with one more burst of assured ignorance. Thomas thinks he's seen the real purpose behind Jesus' statements. They must all go with Jesus to face death bravely. He leaps to the conclusion that Jesus wants them to march unflinchingly into danger [v.16]. He's as heroic as an actor auditioning for the role of a soldier volunteering for a desperate mission. Thomas's blithe missing of the point might remind readers of Andrew's more hapless response to Jesus' question about finding food (see 6:4). Here, once again, a disciple sees, interprets, and defines a situation from his own narrow perspective—and gets it wrong.

JESUS ASKS MARTHA IF SHE BELIEVES [JN.11:17–31]

[17] *As Jesus entered Bethany, he learned Lazarus had been in the tomb for four days.* [18] *Bethany was near Jerusalem, about two miles away.* [19] *And many Jews had come [from Jerusalem] to Martha and Mary to console them at the death of their brother.* [20] *When Martha heard Jesus was near, she went to meet him. Mary stayed home.* [21] *Martha said to Jesus, "Lord, if you'd been here, my brother wouldn't have died.* [22] *Still, I know that whatever you ask God, God will give you."* [23] *"Your brother will rise," said Jesus.* [24] *"I know he'll rise in the resurrection of the last day," she said.* [25] *Jesus said, "I am the resurrection. I am the life. If you believe in me, you will live—even if you die.* [26] *All who live, and believe in me, will never die. Do you believe this?"*

[27] *"Yes, Lord," she said. "I've believed you're the Messiah, the Son of God; the one coming into the world."* [28] *After she'd said that, she went quietly to call her sister, Mary. She said, "The Teacher's here. He's asking for you."* [29] *As soon as she heard this, she got up at once and headed off to him.* [30] *Jesus hadn't*

come into the village yet. He was still where Martha had met him. ³¹ *When the Jews who'd come from Jerusalem to console Mary saw her leave the house quickly, they presumed she was going to the tomb to weep. They followed her.*

———◦◦◦———

Here John captures the unfocused commotion that often surrounds grief—a commotion that contrasts with Jesus' calm. Martha goes out to Jesus [v.20] and speaks vaguely of what she thinks might have been [v.21] and what still might be [v.22]. She says she knows about the promise of a final resurrection [v.24] (learned, perhaps, from what she's heard from the scriptures—see Is.2:2; Mi.4:1; Dan.12:2–3). She expresses some belief in Jesus as God's Anointed One [v.27] but seems anxious to return to her sister—and to send her to Jesus [v.28]. Mary, like Martha, bolts from the house [v.29], setting the curious crowd off in pursuit [v.31]. In the midst of all this movement, Jesus stays in one place. And he says, in effect, one thing: "Do you believe what I've been saying about God sharing his life with us?"

John reminds us that Lazarus, Martha, and Mary are Jesus' friends who know him as a teacher [v.28]. They've heard what he's tried to teach all his disciples—and every other listener. Recall how Jesus tried to get the multitude who'd been fed bread and fish to imagine that God's promise to give them eternal nourishment was not only true but was also being fulfilled at that moment (see 6:39–40). But that well-fed multitude was distracted by the dream of free food. Here, Jesus is talking to people distracted by grief. In both cases, we see people wishing life could be as they'd like it to be— not as God has created it. Martha's answer to Jesus' question about believing [v.26] could be rephrased as: "No, not yet."

JESUS AGAIN GIVES THANKS TO THE FATHER, SO THE CROWD MIGHT BELIEVE [JN.11:32–44]

³² *When Mary came up to Jesus, she looked at him, and she fell at his feet. She said, "Lord, if you'd been here, my brother wouldn't have died."* ³³ *When Jesus*

saw she was weeping, and that the Jews who'd followed her were also weeping, he was upset deep in his soul. ³⁴ He asked them, "Where have you laid him?" They said, "Lord, come see." ³⁵ Jesus wept. ³⁶ Some said, "See, he cared for him." ³⁷ Some others said, "Wasn't this one able to open the eyes of a blind man? Couldn't he have prevented this man's death?" ³⁸ Again, Jesus was deeply distressed. He came to the tomb, a cave with a stone across the entrance. ³⁹ He said, "Take the stone away." Martha said, "Lord, it's been four days. He'll stink." ⁴⁰ "Didn't I say that if you believed, you'd see the glory of God?" ⁴¹ So, they lifted away the stone. Jesus lifted up his eyes. He said, "Father, I give thanks that you've heard me. ⁴² I know you always hear me, but I say it now so the crowd standing here may believe you sent me." ⁴³ Then, with a full voice, he called, "Lazarus, come out." ⁴⁴ The one who died came out, wrapped with a grave cloth from his arms to his feet, and a cloth about his face. "Unbind him," Jesus told them. "Let him go."

———❧❧❧———

What could be simpler? If you believed God's glory was at work in you [v.40], and if you gave thanks because God is always attending closely to you [v.42], why would you fear the prospect of your own death, or the grief that comes from the death of someone you love?

Mary's tears and the weeping of the mourners arouse in Jesus an intense distress [v.33]. This, it seems to me, is because their crying isn't just an expression of personal loss. It's also a cry of personal disappointment. They feel that Jesus has let them down. As some in the crowd say, he should have been able to prevent Lazarus's death [v.37].

Note that, when Jesus weeps [v.35], his tears are a response to the crowd's invitation to come and see where Lazarus lies dead [v.34]. He's not an insensitive machine; and he's not pretending to be human. He has some sense of what Lazarus suffered in his dying. His human feelings, fears, pleasures, hopes, and disappointments are part of who he is—the Son of Man, the Savior, Messiah, Teacher, and one of us. And precisely because he is one of us, he wants us to know that, like him, when we are moved to tears by grief, we can continue to trust that our tears will be wiped away. He invites us to see God's glory even in the face of death: raise your eyes to heaven, give thanks to God, and believe.

REJECTING BELIEF; SEEKING DEATH [JN.11:45–57]

⁴⁵ Some of the Jews who'd come from Jerusalem to console Mary saw what Jesus did, and they believed in him. ⁴⁶ Some others, however, went to the Pharisees and reported what he did. ⁴⁷ So the chief priests and the Pharisees gathered together the whole Sanhedrin—that is, the authorities of the Official Council. They put this case: "What should we do? This man accomplishes many signs. ⁴⁸ If we let this go on, everyone will believe in him. Then the Romans will destroy the Temple—the whole people!" ⁴⁹ Caiaphas stood up. He was the high priest that year. He said, "You don't know what you're saying. ⁵⁰ You're not thinking! Who should perish—one man, or the people?" ⁵¹ These words weren't just his own. His prophetic powers as high priest let him say the truth—that Jesus would die for the people. ⁵² But not just for the people of God. He would die to bring together all God's scattered children. ⁵³ From that moment on, they kept planning a way to kill him. ⁵⁴ So Jesus no longer moved openly among his fellow Jews. He traveled north with his disciples into the wilderness, to a small place called Ephraim. ⁵⁵ But as another Passover approached, many pilgrims went up to Jerusalem from their towns in the countryside to purify themselves before the feast began. ⁵⁶ They looked for Jesus as they milled about the Temple, and they gossiped, "Do you think he'll dare come to the feast?" ⁵⁷ By this time, the chief priests and the Pharisees had issued commands that anyone who knew Jesus' whereabouts should reveal that information and facilitate his arrest.

—————

From the beginning of this Gospel, John has described mixed responses to Jesus. Some people have believed him, but others have reacted to him with surprise, hesitation, and doubt. (These included some of the first disciples. Recall Nathanael's cheekiness—see 1:46.) In these scenes, the contrast among the different responses is starker than ever before. Some want to believe Jesus [v.46]; some want him arrested [v.47a]; some want him dead [vv.50, 53]. This hodgepodge of opinion, ranging from mild interest to lethal hostility, makes it dangerous for Jesus to keep teaching. So he withdraws [v.54]. When people conjectured about the likelihood of Jesus returning to Jerusalem [v.56], they may have reached the sensible conclusion that they'd seen the last of him.

But John has not pictured Jesus doing things that seem sensible to others, but doing what makes sense to the Father. He's God's Son and delights in doing what his Father wants. The startling irony John drops into the middle of this scene is that the high priest—a practical politician—also chooses to do what God wants: let Jesus die for the people of God. The high priest's words about keeping the whole people from perishing [v.50] may be sincere, or they may be his way of saying he's afraid that, if people make too much noise about Jesus, the occupying Romans will take control of Jerusalem away from the Jewish authorities—in which case, the power of the Jewish authorities would perish. Better Jesus should pass away than their power be taken away. Jesus, of course, will pass away not to keep power, but to let it go.

Jesus' choice is elegantly simple. He has taught that the Father doesn't want us to become slaves to darkness and death, but wants us to have eternal life and glory. Nonetheless, fear of death and bodily harm distracts everyone Jesus meets. (Recall the anxieties Jesus confronted in just the last few episodes: the mourning for Lazarus [11:14], the danger faced by a flock of sheep [10:7–18], and the fear of the newly seeing man's parents [9:20–23].) Jesus' teaching hasn't erased people's dread of suffering and death. Despite all he's said, the people to whom he speaks still can't imagine that dying could be part of God's gift of life. They do not want to die. So the Father's simple plan is to let Jesus die for them. He will do this in such a way that God's glory will be revealed in his action. It's as simple as saying to someone who holds an enormous key ring on which the right key seems hard to find, "Here, let me do that for you." "Ah," says the frustrated searcher as the helping hand opens the door, "*that* key! Thank you." If someone unlocks a door for us in this fashion, we're comforted to see there is, indeed, a key—though we had been ready to suppose we would never find it. The door looks different to us now. We can open it.

Once Jesus dies for us and we discover through his resurrection that life doesn't stop at death, we can begin to imagine death just as he does. We can begin to give the same witness about death and life that he does. When we let others see our trust that, through death, we enter into full life, we offer our dying as a lesson—we die for others.

TWELVE

Jesus Returns to Friends in Bethany; Faces Threats in Jerusalem

JESUS' DINNER WITH FRIENDS CAUSES MIXED FEELINGS
[JN.12:1–11]

[1] *Six days before the feast of Passover, Jesus traveled to Bethany, where Lazarus had been raised from death.* [2] *They had a dinner for Jesus: Martha served; Lazarus reclined at table with Jesus and the others.* [3] *Holding half a kilogram of expensive oil scented with imported nard, Mary anointed Jesus' feet, then wiped his feet with her hair. The house filled with fragrance.* [4] *Judas Iscariot spoke up. He was the disciple who was about to betray Jesus' whereabouts [to the authorities].* [5] *"Why wasn't that oil sold? It would have netted a year's salary—which could have been given to the poor."* [6] *The poor didn't matter to him. He spoke this way because he was a thief who took what he wanted out of the common money box.* [7] *Jesus said, "Let her be. She's saved it for my burial day.* [8] *You always have the poor. You don't always have me."* [9] *A large crowd heard of Jesus' presence there. They had gathered not just to see Jesus but also out of curiosity to see the one he raised from the dead—Lazarus.* [10] *[The authorities had also heard about the raising.] So the chief priests decided to kill Lazarus too* [11] *because, on account of him, Jews were coming to believe in Jesus.*

⸺◦◦◦⸺

Here John describes an idyllic moment shared by Jesus and his friends: an intimate dinner; the pleasures of an aromatic foot rub; wafting perfume [vv.1–3]. He then breaks the mood with Judas' complaint about self-indulgence [vv.4–5]. The irony is heavy as Judas, the sticky-fingered treasurer, lectures Jesus about others' needs [v.6]. Beneath this surface irony lies a deeper paradox. From John's description, it seems that Jesus believes in the pleasures of this life as much as he believes in the pleasures of divine life. For him, life in this God-created world is not a prelude to another kind of life. This, right now, is God's life, and Jesus takes delight in it. It also seems evident from this scene that Judas is not delighted by life. He's a testy thief whose attempts to improve his lot by grabbing other people's money haven't made him happy. The paradox here is that Jesus—who seems pleased with life—is ready to lay it down (see 10:11–18), while Judas, who seems unhappy with his lot, grabs at life. Who has more joy?

Although this pleasant scene of enjoying one's friends is interrupted by others, it still manages to be touched with joy—even humor. Jesus comments wryly about the fact that perfumed oil, while good for a massage, is also necessary at a burial [v.7]. His lightness in referring to death doesn't diminish its seriousness. His matter-of-factness contrasts with the pompous solemnity with which Judas speaks of the poor. Judas refers to them (as many people do) as a serious human problem being overlooked by others. Jesus suggests (not too subtly but nonetheless gently) that Judas will always have time to address the needs of the poor. Meantime, he might consider paying attention to a more pressing need: he should listen to Jesus because he's right here speaking the truth to him about life [v.8].

If the atmosphere of this idyll isn't marred by Judas, it certainly seems to be broken by the arrival of the curiosity seekers John describes [v.9]. This crowd wants to see the result of one of Jesus' wonders: Lazarus redivivus. John doesn't mention what precisely they thought they'd see. (Maybe they wanted to brag: "I once saw a man sitting up who'd been dead four days. He was eating dinner, and talking with the man who'd called him from the grave.") Whatever they may have wanted, John certainly doesn't suggest it was the glory of God—the only thing Jesus' signs are intended to reveal. Like the crowds Jesus encountered on his first visit to Jerusalem (2:23–25), and the well-fed crowd who pursued him across a lake (6:26–27), Lazarus's nosy neighbors don't seem interested in anything deeper than the surface wonder of Jesus' works. Their curiosity is apparently stalled at the question, "How did he do that?" They're not ready for the only answer Jesus has given to their question: "These are my Father's works."

As described by John, the chief priests' view of life is even bleaker than the dismal short-sightedness of Judas and the onlookers at the dinner. All they can see is a threat to their power. They believe they have the responsibility and authority to shape people's lives. From their anxious and fretful perspective, nothing could be worse than losing their power to the Romans (see 11:48–50). It's obvious to them that, to protect themselves—or, as they claim, to protect the people—they must arrange a death. This sort of twisted and deadly logic is inevitable when we look at the life God is creating for eternity, and insist that the most important part of that life is the part we see right now.

JESUS DARES TO ENTER JERUSALEM [JN.12:12–19]

12 The next day, the pilgrims who had come to the feast of Passover heard that Jesus was heading into Jerusalem. 13 They took branches from palms and went out to meet him. They chanted Psalm verses: "Hosanna [i.e., 'Lord, bring us salvation']. Blessed is the one who comes in the Lord's name" [Ps.118:25–26]. [And they cried:] "Blessed be the king of Israel." 14 Jesus came across a young donkey. He sat on it. Scripture pictures this [in the Book of Zechariah]. 15 "Do not fear, Zion's daughter. Look, your king is coming. He rides the foal of a donkey" [Zec.9:9]. 16 The disciples didn't understand any of this at the time. After Jesus was glorified, however, they understood how the scripture and the actions of the crowd fit together. 17 And the people who had been there when Jesus called Lazarus from the tomb and raised him from the dead kept giving testimony [to that miracle]. 18 It was on account of hearing that testimony that the visiting pilgrims went out to meet him. [19] *The Pharisees said, "See? No one shares our view. The whole world goes after him."*

John emphasizes that the pilgrims who rushed out to meet Jesus did so because they'd heard about his extraordinary powers—in particular, that he had raised Lazarus from the dead [vv.17–18]. They were taking his approach to Jerusalem as an opportunity to celebrate his wonder working, and to demonstrate that sensational accomplishments were just what they were looking for in a king [v.13]. Earlier, John described Jesus thwarting a boisterous crowd's intention to make him their king because they marveled at his power to give them bread (see 6:15). Here, he describes Jesus reacting to the crowd's shouts of "King of Israel!" by choosing to ride on a donkey. John then cites the Book of the Prophet Zechariah to suggest that Jesus was reminding the crowd of a different sort of king—the sort described in Zechariah, where a king rides on a donkey rather than a war horse, and unites all nations in peace. To appreciate Jesus' action as a good lesson, we don't have to imagine everyone in the crowd immediately picking up on his reference to Zechariah. His behavior said, "Yes, I am a king; but keep watching to see what kind of king I am" [vv.14–15].

When John tells us that the disciples didn't understand Jesus' actions until later [v.16], the reader is encouraged to think ahead to the triumph Jesus reveals in the resurrection—the triumph of God's glory and life overpowering our notion of death and defeat. Then John highlights the fact that the excited pilgrims didn't rethink their desire for a powerful, wonder-working leader [v.17]. Instead, they waged a political campaign on Jesus' behalf, broadcasting again and again the proof of his marvelous powers: he raised Lazarus from death [v.7]. And as we've seen (see 11:51), the authorities felt threatened by any signs of power other than those they wielded themselves [vv.18–19].

Once more John has portrayed Jesus providing a simple lesson. Jesus' actions remind anyone who is paying attention that the glory

God has been planning to share with us from the beginning will look like God's idea of glory. This lesson carries the warning that, every time we grab at what we think is glorious, we'll be left holding nothing. The pilgrims at the feast of Passover, obviously impressed by the story of the raising of Lazarus, shouted their approval of a man who seemed able to work wonders. How delirious they must have felt with their good luck; here was a man who could fulfill their dreams. They were close to the truth: Jesus *is* filled with the power of divine life. But their cries of hosanna—"Save us!"— suggest they may have been looking for something more immediate than the promise of eternal life.

GREEKS WANT TO MEET JESUS; JESUS EMBRACES GLORY; THE CROWD IS UNCERTAIN [JN.12:20–36]

[20] Some Greek speakers were attending the feast along with all the others who'd come up to Jerusalem to worship. [21] They approached Philip—who was from Bethsaida, near Galilean territory. They made this request: "Sir, we'd like to meet Jesus." [22] Philip mentioned the request to Andrew. Then the two of them brought it to Jesus. [23] This was Jesus' response: "This is now the hour for the Son of Man to be glorified. [24] O, yes; O, yes. O yes, indeed, I say that unless a kernel of wheat tossed on the ground dies, it just lies there. But, if it dies, it yields abundant fruit. [25] Whoever loves this life loses life. Whoever hates this life embraces life eternal. [26] Does someone wish to serve me—attend to me? Let that person follow me. Where I am, there too is the one who serves me. The Father will honor whoever serves me. [27] Yes, I'm unsettled in my soul. But should I say, 'Father, save me from this hour'? This is what the hour is for [i.e., to face death, yet still find glory]. [28] Father, glorify your name." A voice answered from heaven: "Glorify? I have. I will." [29] The crowd said they heard thunder. Others said, "No, an angel spoke to him." [30] Jesus told them, "The voice wasn't for me, but for you. [31] This world is being judged. The leader of this world is being cast aside. [32] When I am lifted up from the earth, I will draw all to myself." [33] He was talking about how he would die. [34] In response, the crowd said, "Scripture tells us God's anointed will be with us always [see, e.g., Ps.89:36–37]. What's this about the Son of Man being lifted away—what sort of 'Son of Man' is this?" [35] Jesus said, "You only

have the light for a while. Go your way in that light before the dark catches you.
You don't know where you're walking when you walk in darkness. ³⁶ You have
light. Trust it. Become children of the light." After this last attempt to teach,
Jesus kept silent.

John doesn't mention whether the Greek speakers were Greek-
speaking Jews from somewhere else in the empire or pious Gentiles
who, seeking more nourishment than they found in the rituals of
the state religion, were visiting Jerusalem in their quest. Nor does
John say why they sought Jesus. All we hear is that they approached Philip, perhaps because of his Greek name, and asked to
meet Jesus [vv.20–21]. Neither does John say why Philip didn't go
straight to Jesus with the request [v.22]. But by putting this slight
hitch in the narrative, John has added a hint of formality where
none has existed before. People have been walking directly up to
Jesus since he first appeared on the scene. Recall the Baptist pointing him out, and Andrew approaching him—without introduction—to ask where he was staying (see 1:38).

John's description of Jesus' succinct response seems to be a de-
liberate contrast to the roundabout request. He says quite simply
that the time has come for glory—no more hesitating [v.23]. We can
imagine the Greeks hearing this response, or we may suppose that
only Philip and Andrew were present. Or we can picture the Greeks
and the two disciples coming up to Jesus while he was still surrounded by the excited people who acclaimed his approach to Jerusalem [12:12]. It doesn't matter. As is always the case in John's descriptions of Jesus speaking, here too he goes directly to a basic
question: What are you looking for? Jesus has repeatedly said what
the answer should be: I am looking for divine life and glory. Despite
the fact that Jesus has revealed God's glory many times (e.g., at
Cana, at the Sheep Pool, in the man born blind, in the raising of
Lazarus), people still don't see the glory of God. They haven't taken
to heart Jesus' repeated assurances that his Father—their Father—
has been at work.

Now is the time for Jesus to begin the lesson that will sum up his previous lessons and reveal at last, even to his dimmest disciples, the glory of God. As is true of Jesus' other lessons, this one is simple—as simple as noticing how grass grows. If a kernel of wheat lies on the ground without dying into the next stage of growth, it's just an isolated seed in a casing. But if it dies, it blossoms into a bounty of life. So take your choice: lie there encased in your narrow view of life; or let go of your bonds and live [vv.24–25]. Jesus is addressing the curious Greeks, his disciples, and anyone inclined to believe in him when he says, "If you want to learn from me, you'll have to follow me. And after hearing what I just said about dying and living, where do you suppose I'm going? Yes, death. But fear not. If you follow me into death, who will you find there? You will find the Father waiting to share eternal life with us—to crown us with glory [v.26].

John tells us Jesus didn't pretend that trusting the Father was easy. He describes him speaking about what he sees waiting for him and for those who follow him into death. First, he says, you'll struggle with horror—as he does [v.27a]. But after reflecting on what he should do in the midst of his agony [v.27b], he decides to call on the Father and ask him to reveal his glory [v.28a]. This is perfect for the Father, because he wants to say yes; so Jesus asks [v.28b]. Then John describes the sort of disagreement we've seen before: some people explain a puzzling sound by explaining it away; but some wonder if God might be at work through an angel [v.29]. Jesus asks them to hear God speaking directly to them about glory. Because God has promised to care for them, of course they should expect the deadly forces of this world to be overcome [v.31]. And they should trust Jesus, whom God sent to bring them to glory, to do so [v.32]. John then reminds us that Jesus' being "lifted up" to glory was going to happen literally—in death [v.33]. (And recall what Jesus has said before about being "lifted up"—see 3:14; 8:28.)

This teaching moment follows the same pattern as previous lessons. Once again Jesus' listeners let their preconceptions obscure Jesus' simple images. Like the authorities who couldn't fit John the Baptist into their notions about the One to Come (see 1:19–25), the people here can't rethink their assumptions about the sort of leader they want. Although they have recently greeted Jesus as a mighty king, they can't accept Jesus' description of a different sort of leader. They've read their scripture, and they're sure what it means [v.34a]. They're so constrained by their idea of a permanent kingdom presided over by a long-lived leader that they scoff at Jesus' expression, "lifted up," because they've jumped to the conclusion it means "taken away." As for "the Son of Man," they treat it as a riddle that Jesus should unravel for them [v.34b].

John puts the title "Son of Man" in the mouths of the crowd. By doing so, he seems to suggest they're frustrated by Jesus' use of terms and titles in ways that don't fit their expectations. They might as well be saying, "Why do you keep telling us what we don't want to hear?" They're not ready to reflect that Jesus might simply be saying: "the Father wants a human being—a son of a man—who is willing to be lifted up to glory so that all other humans can follow his example. I am that Son of Man."

Jesus concludes his teaching with a plea that's also a warning. His listeners mustn't keep ignoring these lessons. They should open up to his words while he's still there to enlighten them. Otherwise, they'll wander around in the dark they've created for themselves. Jesus begs them not to become lonely, benighted orphans, but glorious, light-filled children of God [v.36a].

JOHN PUTS JESUS' FAILURE INTO THE CONTEXT OF SCRIPTURE [JN.12:37–43]

[37] Jesus' many signs hadn't led people to believe in him. [38] This fulfilled what the prophet Isaiah said, "Lord, who believed what they heard? To whom has the arm of the Lord been revealed?" [Is.53:1]. [39] The reason they couldn't believe was also expressed by Isaiah: [40] "He's blinded their eyes and hardened their hearts so that they may not see with the eyes or feel with the heart, and turn, and I heal them" [Is.6:10]. [41] Isaiah said this because he saw Jesus' glory and spoke about it. [42] [We have to note that,] even among the Jewish authorities, there were many who believed in Jesus. But they didn't admit this openly. They feared the Phari-

sees and expulsion from the synagogue. ⁴³ They preferred human glory to the glory of God.

John has depicted an almost unbroken string of failures for Jesus as a teacher. Although Jesus' words have moved many, and many have marveled at his miracles, people's willingness to trust his message and act on his words has been feeble. His proclamation of the Good News has elicited, at best, the sort of half-hearted responses John refers to here [vv.42–43]. Now John puts this failure in the context of other prophetic rejections.

By telling us that Jesus now kept silent—or "hid himself"—John tells us that Jesus knew he was in danger (see just above, v.36b). How did things get so bad? True, the author warned us at the beginning that Jesus would be rejected by his own people [1:11]. But why did this happen? To answer this, John cites the words of Isaiah. He might also have quoted from other authors of prophetic literature. The scriptures report that prophetic pronouncements repeatedly fell on deaf ears or, worse, provoked anger. Prophets were not believed [v.38]. But John doesn't simply repeat the confounding fact that the people of God ignored the prophets' reminders about God's words and preferred listening to themselves. He makes the astounding point that it is God who has blinded eyes and hardened hearts to his own word [v.40]—and to Jesus' word as well [v.39]. The rejection of Jesus' message, says John, was an outcome that Isaiah foresaw and described [v.41]. He doesn't say precisely where Isaiah gives this description. But we can suppose that, because Isaiah says he is not worthy to proclaim God's word (see Is.6:5), he imagined a day when someone would appear who *was* worthy—a glorious, perfect embodiment of the divine Word. And we can also suppose that, because Isaiah seems to be a realist, he could sense that even a perfect expression of God's word would be ignored. By reminding us of Isaiah's words, John suggests that Jesus' failure was part of God's plan.

That may sound as perverse as giving a deaf person a radio. If God allows people to be hard-hearted and resistant to learning, what result other than failure can he expect when he tries to teach? John has already suggested the answer to that question in the story of Jesus' cure of the blind man. Recall that the newly seeing man realized he had a blindness that was deeper than simple sightlessness (see 9:35–39). Rather than pretend this was not so, he acknowledged his need for more light. He didn't harden his heart to the fact that he was in deeper darkness than physical blindness. And he was happy to turn to God for the light he needed. The Pharisees, however, were unwilling to consider any possibility that they too might be suffering from profound blindness. They refused to see themselves as creatures who needed and would always need divine light. Their hard hearts kept them in sinful separation from God (see 9:40–41). Here John is reminding us that we must be willing to look for God for the help—the light—we need, but that God will let us harden our hearts and remain in darkness if that's our choice.

John ends this section with the depressing fact that there were some people in positions of power who were inclined to believe in Jesus, but kept from doing so because their desire for the approval of their bullying superiors—with whom they didn't agree—was greater than their longing for God's gift of glory [vv.42–43].

JESUS' SOLILOQUY ABOUT TEACHING [JN.12:44–50]

44 Jesus spoke out loud: "Those who believe in me are putting trust not in me but in the Father who sent me. 45 Those who see me, see the one who sent me. 46 I come to the world as light. All who believe need no longer be in darkness. 47 I don't pass judgment on one who hears my teaching but doesn't accept it. I haven't come to pass judgment on the world, but to save the world. 48 Those who reject me and drown me out already have a judge. My word will be their judge on the last day. 49 That's because I don't speak for myself. The one who sent me, the Father, has commanded what should be told and retold. 50 I know his command is that we are to live eternally [with him]. So, of course I say what the Father told me to say."

There's no note from the author to suggest where Jesus might be speaking these words. The fact that he's been described in hiding [v.36b] allows us to picture him speaking to some disciples who share his seclusion, or to imagine him reflecting aloud to himself. The setting is less important than the fact that John is giving the reader a chance to overhear Jesus' reflections about his work as a teacher.

First, Jesus affirms what he's repeatedly told others about his message: it's not his; it's the Father's [vv.44–45]. Then he says the purpose of the Father's works and words in him is enlightenment [v.46], not censure or indictment [v.47a]. The Father doesn't want people to perish in their sinfulness but to be saved from it [v.47b]. He says those who persist in rejecting his Good News should imagine the last day, and picture how their words will measure up against his words [v.48]—words he spoke because they were the words of God [v.49]. Finally, he says it should be obvious he wants to say the things God says—especially because God says this: "I would like to share my divine life with you forever and ever" [v.50]. Who wouldn't want to hear such a thing?

THIRTEEN

Jesus and His Disciples Together for a Supper

JESUS WASHES HIS DISCIPLES' FEET [JN.13:1–15]

¹ It wasn't long before the feast of Passover that Jesus knew his hour had come—the moment for him to pass from this world to the Father. Because he loved those who'd given themselves to him, he loved them to the end. ² They were having supper. And the devil, the one who leads the heart astray, had already moved the heart of Judas Iscariot, son of Simon, to betray Jesus. ³ But Jesus knew the Father had put everything in his hands; he knew he came from God, he knew he was going to God. ⁴ So he got up. He took off his long robe. He wrapped a towel around his waist. ⁵ He poured water into a big bowl, washed the disciples' feet, and dried them with the towel wrapped around his waist. ⁶ Up he came to Simon Peter, who said, "You wash my feet, Lord?" ⁷ Jesus answered, "You don't understand now what I'm doing, but you will." ⁸ Peter said, "You'll never wash my feet." Jesus said, "If I don't, you'll have nothing to do with me." ⁹ "Lord," said Peter, "not just the feet, then, but the hands too, and the head." ¹⁰ Jesus said, "Someone who's bathed needs only a foot bath; he's already clean. You're all clean. No. Not all." ¹¹ He knew who was betraying him, so he said, "Not all are clean." ¹² After Jesus washed the disciples' feet, he robed himself and reclined once more. He said, "Do you know what I've done? ¹³ You call me 'the Teacher,' 'the Lord.' That's right. I am. ¹⁴ If I, 'the Teacher,' 'the

Lord,' washed your feet, you should wash each other's feet. [15] *I gave you an example. Do what I did."*

—⟨⟨⟨∘⟩⟩⟩—

When we read that Jesus knew his hour had come [v.1a], we may wonder how he knew. If we have a twitch of puzzlement in response to John's description of Jesus' knowledge, we might recall that he's repeatedly described a similar puzzlement in Jesus' audiences—and in his disciples. As the supper scene unfolds, John again contrasts human puzzlement and anxiety with Jesus' trust and confidence in his Father. He invites us to accept the fact that Jesus not only knows the difference between his desires and God's desires, but he also knows how to choose correctly between them. This is nothing new in John's narrative. Jesus' teaching has been an extended conversation about the possibility of giving oneself completely to the God who gives himself completely to you. John has described the Jewish authorities as shocked by Jesus' claim of such intimacy with God. But he has also depicted Jesus' family, friends, disciples, and various audiences as reluctant to enter into this conversation with an open mind. Recall Nicodemus (3:9–10), the Samaritan woman (4:12), the well-fed crowd (6:42), Jesus' brothers (7:5), the parents of the man born blind (9:20–23), Jesus' friends Martha (11:21) and Mary (11:32), and the frequent second-guessing of his disciples. All these people are described as worried and confused.

Jesus too has been described as fearful and unsettled at heart. We read that, soon after the crowds greeted him with palms, he spoke of his deep anxiety about his approaching "hour" (12:27). But we also read that he didn't let his troubled heart set his course of action for him. Instead, he chose to let the Father continue the work of giving him divine glory (12:28). Jesus is about to show his disciples how they too can choose to do the Father's will rather than their own.

It's a simple lesson of service, and John sets it up succinctly. First, he notes that, at this moment of passing from the world, Jesus' attention wasn't on himself, but on those he loved. Yes, at this moment, though Jesus is confident he's going to the Father, he doesn't luxuriate selfishly in thoughts of release. He's not like a child on the last day of school straining every nerve to hear the bell that will launch him to freedom. Rather, his attention is on his disciples and their needs [v.1b]. Because of John's mention of the devil's work, it may seem that this is a moment of defeat [v.2]. But he then describes Jesus doing what he always does in response to rejection. He gives an example of comfort and care. On this occasion, he washes his disciples' feet [vv.4–5].

Peter is described as confounded by what he sees as an inappropriate reversal of roles. Because Jesus is "Lord," he shouldn't be washing feet [vv.6, 8a]—he shouldn't be serving. Jesus, a teacher who is always patient, asks Peter to be ready to learn something different from what he thinks is right [vv.7, 8b]. John may be having a bit of fun at Peter's expense when he describes his self-dramatizing offer to submit to a fuller washing [v.9]. But, comic or not, Peter's grandstanding is one more example of the disciples' habit of misunderstanding Jesus' simple lessons—a habit that could be deadly, as John reminds us, when he reports Jesus' words about the betrayal [vv.10–11]. As if to point out the simplicity of this lesson in serving, Jesus speaks with the simple directness of a salesman: "Try it; you'll see how much you like it." We hear Jesus instructing his disciples to explore the possibility that, if he, their master teacher— their "Lord"—finds satisfaction in serving, the same might be true for them [vv.13–15].

JESUS EXPLAINS SERVICE [JN.13:16–20]

[16] *After Jesus gave the example of washing feet, he said, "O, yes. O, yes. O yes, indeed, I say no slave is greater than his master. Someone who's been sent isn't greater than the sender.* [17] *You may know these truths. You'll be happy only when you act on them.* [18] *Now I'm going to say something that's not meant for you all. I know those I've chosen. Understand what scripture says: 'The friend I trusted—the friend I ate with—now shows me the sole of his shoe' [Ps.41:10].*

¹⁹ Before things start to unfold, I want you to believe what's really unfolding. I am [what's unfolding]. ²⁰ O, yes; O, yes. O yes, indeed, I say when someone accepts you, they accept me. And who am I? I'm the same as the one who sent me. So, if they receive you, they receive me—and they receive the one who sent me."

John tells us Jesus warned his disciples of the danger of thinking they already understood his lessons. Of course they would say, if asked, that they were his students and he was their teacher. But do they understand they're in the middle of a long process of learning? Or are they tempted to say, "Oh, of course we know that"? We hear Jesus inviting them to experience the joy and true happiness—the blessedness—that springs from living what one knows by attempting to put it into action [vv.16–17]. John doesn't spell out the possible frustration in this choice: the more we act on what we know, the more we discover how inadequate our knowledge is. This realization could launch us into more learning, but that would lead us into more actions that would reveal a need to learn still more. This process of repeatedly discovering how little you know will be experienced as happiness only if you're willing to be a perpetual learner.

Jesus is then described telling the group that he wants them to consider something unpleasant: betrayal [v.18]. We don't need to assume the disciples knew all the verses of the cited Psalm. But they would know that it, like every Psalm, depicts moments of distress as the perfect times to call out to God for comfort. The Psalm verse will now be "fulfilled" because the truth it proclaims about God's care for us is about to be revealed in Jesus' experience. The disciples will see that it doesn't matter who turns on them and shakes their shoes at them. God will not abandon them. Watch me, says Jesus to all who want to follow him; watch as God's promise comes true in me [v.19]—and in you [v.20].

JESUS EXPLAINS BETRAYAL [JN.13:21–30]

[21] Then Jesus' soul was beset with trouble. He said, "O, yes; O, yes. O yes, indeed, I have to say one of you will betray me." [22] The disciples looked at each other. They couldn't tell whom he meant. [23] Reclining next to Jesus was the disciple for whom he had great affection. [24] So Peter crooked his head to signal this disciple to ask whom Jesus meant. [25] Leaning back toward Jesus' chest, he says, "Lord, who is it?" [26] Jesus says, "The one to whom I'll give a dipped piece of food." Dipping some food, he gave it to Judas, son of Simon the Iscariot. [27] As the food entered him, Satan entered. Jesus told him, "What you do, do quickly." [28] No one else at table knew why he spoke to him. [29] Some assumed that, because Judas was responsible for the money, Jesus had asked him to buy things for the feast, or to distribute something to the poor. [30] He ate the piece of food and went right out. It was night.

Just above, Jesus used a Psalm verse to remind the disciples that a moment of distress shouldn't lead to a sense of defeat. Rather, it's the perfect time to remember God's compassionate presence (13:18). In an earlier scene, Jesus was moved to tears at the thought of Lazarus entering death's darkness (see 11:35). Here, he faces not only the prospect of dying, but the fact that one of his disciples will put him in the hands of people who've threatened to kill him; of course he's troubled. His distress doesn't lead him to complain, however, but to confront the truth [v.21]. Jesus' announcement of the truth presents an opportunity to teach by example.

The disciples are described as so dumbfounded by Jesus' announcement that they do nothing but gape at one another. They seem to be looking for evidence to support Jesus' statement. But they say nothing; they're unsure of themselves [v.22]. Even the disciple who may have been closest to Jesus isn't described as saying anything until he is prodded by Peter's discreet signal [vv.23–24]. (This close or beloved disciple is never named but is commonly referred to as "John" and identified with the author of the Gospel. These conjectures are beside the point of the narrative. If the writer and editors of the Gospel had wanted readers to know more about this man, they would have written more. What's important here, as in every scene in the Gospel, is Jesus' words and behavior as he deals with various people's difficulties in hearing and accepting the Good News.)

Jesus' response to his close friend's question, "Who is it?" [v.25], isn't responded to with a polite charade. He isn't saying, "So as not to make a fuss, I'll just offer the guilty one a bit of food." The moment is much more poignant. It's a chance for Judas to be touched by Jesus—literally and figuratively [v.26]. It's also another opportunity for any disciple who is watching to learn how Jesus behaves. If they've begun to accept Jesus' assurances that all he does, he does because he wants to respond to the Father's desires, they might ask themselves what Jesus' simple gesture of feeding Judas can tell them about God's desires. Judas could have asked himself the same question. Or he could have asked Jesus, "Why do you offer me food?" And he could have guessed Jesus' answer would be something like, "I feed you because I love you."

But that didn't happen. The morsel was just food to Judas, not a sign of love. He'd become attached instead to Satan—the great doubter and naysayer [v.27a]. It's chilling to picture Jesus speeding Judas on his way [v.27b]. However, it makes sense that, if Judas is determined to go his own way, he should leave immediately. Why linger with someone he's rejected? Jesus puts Judas' decision before him starkly: "Act on your choice right now!" The fact that Judas does so is dismaying. How frightening to head into the dark with such stubborn intent [v.30].

This awful moment of acting out a deadly choice is mixed with a bit of bathos—supplied, not surprisingly, by a description of the disciples' reaction. They couldn't understand what was going on [vv.28–29].

JESUS SPEAKS OF LOVE; PETER SPEAKS OF LOYALTY
[JN.13:31–38]

31 After Judas left, Jesus said, "Now, the Son of Man is glorified—made resplendent by sharing God's own glory. 32 The divine glory God shares with him is truly his. It's in him—in him right now. 33 My children, I'm with you only a while. You'll miss me, but remember what I said to the crowd [when the Temple guards tried to arrest me]: 'You can't get yourself to where I'm going' [see 7:33–34]. I repeat this instruction to you now. 34 I also have a new instruction. Love one another. As I've loved you, love one another. 35 People will know you're my disciples if you love one another." 36 Simon, called Peter, said, "Lord, where're you going?" Jesus answered, "I just said: where you can't follow now. You'll follow later." 37 "Why can't I come now, Lord?" asked Peter. "I'd give up my life for you." 38 "You'd give your life?" Jesus asked. "O, yes; O, yes. O yes, indeed, I tell you tomorrow's cock won't crow before you deny me—three times."

The description of Jesus proclaiming God's glory immediately after Judas' exit into the dark might catch some readers by surprise, but it shouldn't. As early as the introduction, John said God's glory has been made visible (1:14). And in his first story about Jesus' work, he said God's glory was revealed in the unlikely circumstance of a wine shortage. Throughout the narrative of this Gospel, we've seen Jesus asking his listeners if they believed what they'd heard from scripture about God's promise to bring creation to perfection—to share divine light, life, and glory. He's also invited people to hear his words and see his works as evidence of God's desire to fill us with divine power. He's reminded them that nothing—certainly not death—will prevent God's desires from being fulfilled. So the authorities' deadly intentions and Judas' decision to abet them can't keep the Son of Man—one of us—from being glorified. In fact, their actions will help to reveal God's glory when it becomes apparent that death has no hold over Jesus. How could it? He shares God's own glory [vv.31–32].

Jesus points out that the completion of his task to reveal God's glory will mean that he will go away [v.33a]. But he tells the disciples not to let his imminent departure drive them to do anything foolish. In particular, they shouldn't trust themselves to concoct a way to follow him [v.33b]. Jesus is repeating the same lesson he's asked them to learn from the beginning: you can't accomplish God's work, but God can accomplish it in you. The way for the disciples to learn this lesson now is to avoid schemes of their own and, instead, to love one another [v.34]. Of course, if the disciples were to follow that instruction, the effort needed to love one another would leave them with little energy to concoct, promote, or argue over their bright ideas. If each of them struggled to think always of others' needs first, and never to become distracted by their private needs, their struggle would give startling evidence to even casual observers that they were students of Jesus [v.35].

Peter's demand to know where Jesus is going [v.36a], interjected right after the command to love, suggests that Peter hasn't heard the command because he's too concerned with following Jesus—despite the fact he's just been told not to. Jesus' response is a reminder that things are being worked out *for* Peter [v.36b]. This isn't good enough. Peter is so full of trust in himself that there's no room left in his heart—or head—for second thoughts or self-awareness [v.37]. Jesus tells him that events will reveal how empty his boasts are [v.38].

FOURTEEN

At Supper, Jesus Teaches about Trust, and Says the Spirit Will Do the Same

JESUS ADVISES THE DISCIPLES TO LET GOD WORK IN THEM
[JN.14:1–14]

¹ [After telling Peter how little he understood himself, Jesus encouraged all the disciples to take heart. He said,] "Don't let your hearts be troubled. Believe in God. And believe in me. ² There are many places in my Father's home. Otherwise, I wouldn't say I'm going to prepare you a place. ³ So, I'll go prepare your place; I'll come back; I'll take you with me; then, you'll be where I am. ⁴ You know the way I'm going." ⁵ "Lord," said Thomas, "We don't know where you're going, so we can't know the way!" ⁶ "I'm the way," said Jesus. "And I'm the truth; and the life. No one comes to the Father except through me. ⁷ If you know me, you'll know the Father. So, you do know him—you've seen him." ⁸ "Lord," said Philip, "show us the Father. That's all we need." ⁹ Jesus said, "I'm this long with you, Philip, and you don't know me? You've seen me; you've seen the Father! How can you say, 'Show us the Father'! ¹⁰ Don't you believe I'm in the Father and the Father's in me? I don't talk about myself, or for myself. It's the Father, abiding in me, who's at work. ¹¹ Believe me: I am in the Father; the Father is in me. Not enough? Then, believe the divine works. ¹² O, yes; O, yes. O yes, indeed, I say the person who believes in me will do the same works I do—no,

117

even greater works. For now I'm going to the Father. [13] And when you ask in my name, I'll answer. So the Father will be glorified in the Son. [14] If you ask in my name for anything, I'll do it."

———◦◦◦———

What's the first thing you would call on Jesus to do? John has already told us the first—and only—thing that's been recommended by Jesus: ask for untroubled hearts. That's what is implied in the direction to believe [v.1]. When the disciples are vexed, anxious, and full of doubt, they should seek the comfort of putting themselves into God's hands. This is the comfort of trusting in Jesus' message of God's love. Unless they suspect Jesus has been misleading them, they should be delighted to imagine how their hearts will feel when he returns and says, "Come with me to the Father!" [vv.2–3]. If Jesus were to spell out his instructions, he might say, "When your hearts are troubled, don't despair. Look forward to— *ask* for—the comfort that I assure you is yours. Don't ask for anything less." But Jesus doesn't say all that. He simply says, "You know the way" [v.4].

Many readers must be grateful that Thomas asked, "What way?" [v.5]. Like Thomas, we need Jesus' simple reminder that the God he calls Father—the God of scripture who is creating all of us as his children—is not like a distant destination. God is not the mysterious object of an arduous quest. He's our Father. Jesus' statement that the disciples know his way to the Father isn't a riddle. He's going the way he's always proceeded. He's gone to his Father—turned to him—in all his needs. What other way would one go to a loving parent besides going directly? There's no secret access code or special map. But Thomas seems to think there is.

Readers might assume that, by this point in the story, the disciples would have learned to trust that Jesus takes seriously his responsibility as their teacher—that he means exactly what he says when he tells them he's not abandoning them [v.3]. With Thomas's outburst, however, John nudges us to notice that trusting isn't easy for them. Thomas isn't ready to let go of the assumption that, as an

adult who feels responsible for giving shape to his own life, he must
be the judge of what choices he should make. So of course he com-
plains that Jesus isn't giving him enough information. This may
seem to be a reasonable complaint. After all, when we make an
agreement that calls for trust, we feel responsible for monitoring the
other party's reliability. "Trust, but verify," we warn each other.
Jesus is trying to teach a different lesson.

In our relationship with God—with the God who has offered us
a Covenant in which he cares for us—we are always children. In our
relationship with Jesus, we are always students. When we act as if
we're independent adults or our own teachers, we step away from
our relationship with God and Jesus. Jesus tells his disciples
throughout this conversation at supper that, like children, they will
always need care. They will always need a teacher—a guide, a shepherd—to remind them where to find care. They needn't fear their
puzzlement or hesitate to ask about life. And they needn't grab for
answers to life's mysteries. Why grab? They are being *brought* to the
fullness of life! Jesus assures them that it's his task to do the bringing—to be the true way to divine life [v.6]. You know me, he says—
you know how I always turn to the Father and abide in his presence. So, if you follow my example, you too will be abiding in the
Father's presence—you see where I abide, so you see where the
Father abides [v.7].

But the evangelist has Philip speak up. He won't trust in promises; he says, "Give me a taste of this future glory and comfort that
I'll get from the Father" [v.8]. Philip is like a careful shopper. He
wants to evaluate the goods for himself. How sensible. Philip
knows how to evaluate the trustworthiness of God! Put that way, of
course, Philip's demand seems ridiculous. But Jesus doesn't ridicule
him. He merely asks him if he truly thinks it makes sense to demand proof from God that his intentions are reliable [v.9].

According to Jesus, the Father is in the middle of a great work in
us human beings. Because Jesus lets God go about this divine work
in him, anyone who sees how Jesus speaks and acts will see this
work in progress. He doesn't use his relationship with the Father
the way a hanger-on might use a connection with a powerful ac-

quaintance to bask in reflected fame. He's not bragging about his important connections. Jesus' desire is simply the same as the Father's desire: "Let God abide in you" [v.10]. Jesus tells the disciples that, if some part of their brain is stuck on the question of how Jesus and the Father can be mutually present to each other, they should put that question aside while they permit themselves to watch what Jesus does [v.11].

In fact, says Jesus, try doing the Father's work yourselves. Because I'm going to the Father, he says, the two of us will be working to make sure that, whatever divine work you do, it will be greater than the works I've done [v.12]. As far as Jesus is concerned, this is not an outrageous assertion. From his point of view, the process is quite simple and logical. He's saying, "I want you to believe the Father is struggling to share his glory with you. So, first, picture me with the Father. Next, imagine crying out to me, 'Remember, you said the Father wanted to give us his glory. Please, ask him to give it to me!' Then, imagine how delighted the Father will be to see me giving you his glory" [v.13]. There's no possibility that he'll refuse such a request [v.14].

THOSE WHO FOLLOW JESUS' INSTRUCTIONS WILL BE FILLED WITH THE SPIRIT [JN.14:15–31]

[15] [After Jesus said he would always answer the disciples' needs, he said:] "If you love me, you'll do what I tell you. [16] Because I will ask him, the Father will send another to comfort you at all times. [17] This will be the True Spirit—the Spirit the world can't take in because it doesn't notice or attend to the Spirit. You know the Spirit because it abides in you—inside you! [18] I'm not leaving you like orphans. I'm always coming to you. [19] Soon, the world won't see me. But you see me because my life is yours. [20] In time, you'll see that, just as I am in the Father, you're in me, and I'm in you. [21] By taking my instruction and following it, you show your love for me. My Father will love whoever loves me. And I will love whoever loves me—to that one, I will reveal who I am." [22] Judas (not the Iscariot) said to Jesus, "Lord, what makes you reveal yourself to us, but not to the world?" [23] So, Jesus [repeating his lesson,] said, "If you love me, you'll hold on to

my word. My Father will love you [for holding on to my word]. The Father and I will come to you; we'll make our abode with you [if you hold on to my word]. ²⁴ Someone who doesn't love me will dismiss my words. Remember, the word you hear isn't mine. It's the word of the one who sent me. ²⁵ I say all this while I still have time with you. ²⁶ But the Father will send you the Spirit of Comfort—the Holy One. The Spirit will teach you everything—will remind you of all I've said to you. ²⁷ I leave you peace. My peace I'm giving to you. I'm not giving you what the world gives as peace. So don't let your hearts trouble you. Don't be timorous. ²⁸ You've heard what I said: I'm going away; [but] I'm coming back. O, how you should rejoice (if you love me) to know I'm going to the Father—the Father who is greater than me. ²⁹ I've spoken before this happens; when it happens, believe. ³⁰ I won't speak with you much longer. Now comes the kingpin of this world. He has nothing to offer me. ³¹ But the world should know that I love the Father and do only what he wants. So get up. Let's go."

Note: as we'll see below, the Gospel of John continues to report further words from Jesus at the supper. Commentators have pointed out that Chapters 15 through 17 were added by a later hand than the original evangelist's. We don't know why the later editor left the words, "So get up. Let's go," but then continued to describe Jesus speaking with his disciples (see 15:1). This is a curious literary mystery, but it needn't distract the general reader. We'll reflect on the announcement of a departure when we get to the next section.

Here, John describes Jesus reminding the disciples that love is expressed in deeds. So if they love him, they'll do what he's just asked them to do [v.15]—that is, trust in him and trust in the Father (see 14:11–14). Because Jesus wants their actions of trust to be a pleasure, not a burden, he assures them that he and the Father will send someone to help them follow his instructions. This will be someone who will comfort them and cheer them on [v.16]. The source of this abiding comfort, says Jesus, is the divine Spirit [v.17a]. This is the Spirit the world ignores—although it's the same Spirit that's constantly breathing the truth from God—the Spirit that will be breathing in them [v.17b]. This is the Spirit that moves in Jesus. Since they'll be sharing the same Spirit, Jesus will always be with them [v.18].

These startling statements may sound too good to be true. Jesus seems to be aware of this when he says that the world will judge from appearances. They'll simply see he's gone. The disciples shouldn't be fooled by appearances. Jesus can't be gone if he's alive in them [v.19]. If they want to avoid being trapped by their own misjudgments, they should continue to study what he taught them. In other words, be like him: he doesn't understand his relationship with the Father as a mere fact, and he doesn't talk about the Father merely the way one speaks of having a famous ancestor. His relationship with the Father is the unfolding reality of who he is [v.20].

Then Jesus reminds the disciples what he's already told them: love expresses itself in actions. He wants them to remember how important it is to give expression to their trust. He says the Father and he delight in being trusted. And he promises to respond to the disciples' trust with his comforting presence [v.21].

Perhaps John worried that he was setting forth Jesus' comforting words too quickly. But for whatever reason, he chooses this point to let a disciple named Judas ask why the "world" will not receive Jesus' teaching [v.22]. John describes Jesus repeating his lesson as an answer to Judas's question. He's saying, "Do you think the Father delights in being with those who listen to me—with those who let him into their hearts as I have [v.23]? What do you think it's like for the Father to have his word flung back at him—to see his son rejected? Those who don't listen to me don't love me—and they refuse to think my words could be from the Father" [v.24]. Jesus' answer to Judas comes down to the truism that the words of the beloved are always fascinating to the besotted lover, while the world in general usually finds them boring.

Then Jesus returns to the comforting news that, though he'll soon be gone, the divine Spirit will continue to teach the disciples [vv.25–26]. Just as he's told them before, they have no need to fear (see, e.g., 6:20). They should be at peace. But they shouldn't confuse his gift of peace with the tranquility the world mistakes for peace [v.27]. No, they'll be truly at peace if they're willing to abandon their anxious worries about their own concerns, and rejoice instead in the concerns of the Father. They should watch how the Father works out the creation story he began long ago. It's a great story—one that Jesus wouldn't think of altering [v.28]. The disciples, Jesus says, need not be worried or distracted by the world's appalling displays of self-importance. The power of this world is nothing but flashy tricks and noisy illusion [v.30]. Jesus wants to give the world his quiet, humble example—because that's what the Father wants [v.31].

FIFTEEN

Jesus Says: You Are Part of Me; I Love You; Love One Another, Not the World

JESUS DESCRIBES THE DISCIPLES' RELATIONSHIP TO
HIM AND THE FATHER [JN.15:1–10]

[1] *[Jesus continued to speak to the disciples with whom he'd had supper.] "I'm the vine—truly. My Father is the vine grower.* [2] *He cuts off all the fruitless branches. All fruitful branches he trims to get more fruit.* [3] *You've been trimmed already—by the word I spoke to you.* [4] *Abide in me; and I in you. A branch can't bear fruit unless it's still on the vine. Neither can you, unless you abide in me.* [5] *I'm the vine. You're the branches. If you abide in me, and I in you, you bear abundant fruit. Cut off from me, you can do nothing.* [6] *If you're not abiding in me, you're like dried branches pruned, cast in fire, and burned.* [7] *If you do abide in me—that is, if my words live in you—then ask whatever you want. It will be done for you.* [8] *This is what glorifies the Father: that you bear much fruit by being my disciples.* [9] *Just as the Father loved me, I loved you. Abide in my love.* [10] *And you'll abide in my love if you carry out my instructions. [Be like me:] I do what the Father instructs me to do, and abide in his love."*

The above words are the beginning of material that's been added on to the supper scene discussed previously (13:1–14:31). The literary questions of how, when, and why the added material was incorporated into the text are richly challenging but, for the general reader, beside the point. Our basic question here is: what picture of the Good News is created by the version of the Gospel we now read? For instance, contemporary readers have become used to referring to all the material in Chapters 13 through 17 as the "supper discourse." However, since nowhere in the added material (gathered into Chapters 15 through 17) is there a reference to eating, must the reader picture the whole discourse unfolding at the supper? Later in this Gospel (see 18:1), Jesus and his disciples will be described leaving the city of Jerusalem and going across a small valley to a garden. One might, then, imagine the words in verse 1 above being said as the group begins to walk to the garden. Or one might imagine them spoken as the group lingers in the supper room.

Anyone who enjoys films could easily envision this moment and those that follow as a sequence of scenes. In one scene, everyone is strapping their sandals on as Jesus develops an image; next, the group is milling about in the supper room while disciples gather lamps or leftovers; later, perhaps Jesus stops in the street to repeat a point; then the group might pause at the Temple for more conversation; or everyone may have stopped to greet disciples who weren't at the supper but want to join the conversation—and so on. No matter how one pictures these moments, it's important to notice that they're part of an extended conversation in which Jesus continues the work he's done from the beginning of the Gospel: he teaches.

Here, we catch Jesus in mid-image, explaining how there's a living connection between him and his disciples. This connection will remain vital and intimate even though Jesus is going away. First, he says, picture a vine [v.1]. Now picture the vine's branches. What makes the branches alive is their connection to the vine [v.2]. Then he asks them to imagine that they've already been prepared to be real extensions of himself—yes, prepared by his word [v.3]. So he says: "Keep my word alive in you" [v.4].

The simplicity of Jesus' message is emphasized when it's restated: "I'm the vine. You're my branches. When we remain connected [by my words], you flourish" [v.5]. The message is then expressed in the negative: "There can't be any connection between you and me without my words. My words are our shared life. Disconnection from my word is death" [v.6]. One further repetition hammers home the point that the disciples should stay connected with Jesus' word: "My words will live and thrive in you just as they have in me. What have you heard me say, and what have you seen me do? Yes, I asked the Father that his works be done in me. I tell you to do the same thing: ask [v.7]. The Father is glorified when you follow my teaching and example [v.8]. (Why? Because others see that you listen to the divine word and find your nourishment in it.) The Father loves you to listen to me [v.9]. Do what I tell you: abide with the Father and me; love as we do" [v.10].

JESUS TELLS THE DISCIPLES TO LEARN TO LOVE [JN.15:11–17]

[11] *"I've been speaking to you like this," said Jesus, "because I want my joy to be inside you. I want your joy to be complete—like mine.* [12] *So, I give you this instruction, this command: love one another as I've loved you.* [13] *You can't have greater love than to give your life for your friends.* [14] *You're my friends, if you act on my instruction.* [15] *Notice I don't call you servants. A servant doesn't know what the Master does. I call you friends because I tell you all the Father tells me.* [16] *You didn't choose me. But I did choose you. I chose you and set you apart to do something—something that will last. Ask the Father, and he'll give you what's lasting.* [17] *My instruction can be summed up in this: love one another."*

Just above, the author described Jesus asking the disciples to love exactly as he and the Father love. That request seems to demand the impossible. We can't love like God. We don't know how. Now the author describes Jesus explaining that this instruction isn't meant to be a burden, but a delight. Jesus wants the disciples to be flooded with the same divine joy that fills him [v.11], so he tells them how to respond to this desire of his: "I give you this instruction: love one another as I've loved you" [v.12].

The first part of verses 12 and 17 are more familiarly known to English speakers as, "This is my commandment" [v.12], and "This I command you" [v.17]. These expressions will no doubt call to mind the Ten Commandments. And that's why I chose a different expression. It's easy to confuse the Bible's description of God giving the commandments to his people with a movie version—say, *The Ten Commandments*. That film depicts terrified refugees cowering before smoke, lightning, and thunder, and hearing a far-off voice much like the voice coming from the man behind the curtain in *The Wizard of Oz*. This Hollywood god issues brusque edicts—and that's that. No such God is described in the Book of Deuteronomy.

The author of Deuteronomy takes pains to say why God's people should hear and obey God's commands—just as Jesus has been described throughout this Gospel saying why his disciples should hear and follow him. The reason is simple, but hard to believe. When you take in God's word, you take in God's life—you take in God. God's words—his commands, pronouncements, promises, statutes, decrees, warnings, admonitions, messages, sounds, and his every breath—are alive. When you hear God's commands and observe them by taking them to heart, you will live [Dt.4:1]. Others will marvel at your wise choice of life [Dt.4:5]. You'll never think of turning right or left to look for different commands, because God's commands make you live and prosper [Dt.5:32–33]. God's commands will become like a melody that you find yourself repeating over and over throughout the day. You'll want to tell your children: "You will love the Lord—*your* God—with all your heart! Why? Because his commands are full of life" [Dt.6:4–7].

The author of this part of John's Gospel here describes Jesus reminding his disciples how the love of God—the God depicted in Deuteronomy—works. He says, "Notice my example. I give my life to you. My life is yours because you're my friends" [v.13]. He goes on to say he'll know they accept his friendship when they act like his friends by trusting his commands and fulfilling his instructions [v.14]. Jesus is then described spelling out for his disciples what he means by calling them "friends." Unlike servants who can't expect masters to share their business secrets with them, friends—that is, friends of the sort Jesus imagines for himself—will share all things in common. Jesus says he's already admitted his friends into the intimate conversation he has with the Father [v.15].

This claim that his disciples are in a plain-spoken, friendly conversation with God may seem as inconceivable as Jesus' claim that he intends to share his joy with them completely [v.11]. Perhaps aware that readers might be stunned by this description of close communion with God, the author describes Jesus explaining how this familiar relationship works. Once again, the explanation is simple. Jesus invited the disciples into this closeness; it wasn't their idea. He wants them to experience God's generosity—God's pouring out of his life—just as he experiences it. So, he sends them out to enjoy this divine bounty—to bring in, if you will, the divine harvest—just as Jesus harvested it. To do this, they should follow the example of Jesus, who asked the Father to fulfill the divine work of creation in him [v.16]. If they behave like this, they'll know what love is [v.17].

THE WORLD HAS A DIFFERENT IDEA OF LOVE [JN.15:18–27]

[18] *"If you discover that the world hates you, remember, it hated me," said Jesus.* [19] *"The world will love you as one of its own only if you're part of it. But I picked you out of the world. You're not part of it. Thus, it hates you.* [20] *Remember what I said to you [after I washed your feet], 'No slave is greater than the master' [13:16]. If they harassed and hounded me, they'll hound and harass you. If they welcomed my word, they'll welcome yours.* [21] *What they do to you, they'll do because of who [I've told them] I am. Yes, I'm saying they don't recognize the one who sent me.* [22] *If I hadn't come [from the one who sent me], they wouldn't be sinning [by rejecting me]. They can't pretend their rejection isn't a sinful choice.* [23] *When they reject and hate me, they reject and hate the Father.* [24] *If I hadn't done [the Father's] great works—which have been different from all other human works—their choice wouldn't be sinful. But they've seen these works and nonetheless have chosen to hate both me and the Father.* [25] *Their Law*

comes true in them—the Law expressed in the Psalm, 'they hate me for no reason' [Ps.69:4]. [26] *When the Spirit of Comfort comes—the True Spirit I promised to send you from the Father [see 14:17, 26]—that Spirit will speak for me and repeat my witness.* [27] *You too will speak for me and bear the same witness, because you're with me from the beginning."*

—∽∾∽—

During the preceding moment in this conversation, the author described the disciples being instructed to love one another. Here they're told how much hate they may meet. Since they won't ever speak or act just for themselves (for instance, it wasn't their idea to love one another), and since they'll always be repeating what Jesus taught them, they should expect to be received as Jesus was received [v.18]. It should be clear to them that, by following Jesus, they're not following the way of the world [v.19]. If Jesus encountered rejection, so will they. If he found welcome, welcome will sometimes be theirs [v.20].

Remember, says Jesus, why people wouldn't receive his message: they didn't believe God was at work in their lives. They didn't believe God is still at work in creation, or that God sent him to bring that work to fulfillment [v.21]. He says his fellow Jews should know better. Scripture, in which they say they believe, tells them how God is always working to bring them into a loving communion with him [v.22]. So, he says, when people reject his message of divine love—when they reject God's word (God's Word)—they reject God [v.23].

The author then has Jesus repeat the assertion that a rejection of him is a rejection of the God who has promised to continue the work of creation. He describes Jesus saying that people had seen the work of the Father in him as they'd never seen it before, but they refused to believe what they saw. This refusal to consider the evidence of God's engagement in their lives is called sin [v.24]. Then the author depicts Jesus pointing out the irony that, though the people of God heard God's word proclaimed to them in scripture, they didn't realize God was speaking to them when they listened to the Psalms [v.25].

Jesus is portrayed here warning anyone who follows him that, like him, they'll meet rejection and failure. But the author doesn't conclude this part of Jesus' instruction on a note of defeat: his disciples needn't dread rebuffs any more than he fears the world's disapproval. Jesus is pictured reminding the disciples that he's promised to send them the same Spirit of God that fills him with comfort and peace [v.26]. That enlightening Spirit, whose inspiration moved Jesus to do and say the things the disciples have witnessed from the beginning, will soon lead them to give a similar witness in their words and deeds [v.27].

SIXTEEN

Another Promise to Send the Spirit; More Words of Encouragement

JESUS SAYS IT'S RIGHT FOR HIM TO GO, AND FOR
THE SPIRIT TO COME [JN.16:1–11]

[Recall what Jesus said above (15:26–27): [26] *"When the Spirit of Comfort comes—the True Spirit I promised to send you from the Father (see 14:17, 26)—that Spirit will speak for me and repeat my witness.* [27] *You too will speak for me and bear the same witness—because you're with me from the beginning."]*

[1] *Jesus said, "I've been telling you all this [about the world's contempt] so that you won't be surprised.* [2] *They'll throw you out of synagogues. The hour nears when those who kill you will think they're serving God.* [3] *They'll be acting in ignorance of both the Father and me.* [4] *I'm telling you this so that, when it happens, you'll remember I told you. I didn't tell you in the beginning because I was here with you.* [5] *But now I'm going to the one who sent me. No one says, 'Where are you going?'* [6] *Instead, your hearts respond to my words with sorrow.* [7] *Yet, truly, it's better that I go. If I don't go, the Spirit of Comfort won't come. If I go, I'll send you the Spirit.* [8] *When the Spirit comes, the Spirit will give the world proof of sin, justice [what's right], and judgment.* [9] *Sin? That they didn't believe in me.* [10] *What's right? I'm going to the Father and you'll see me no more.* [11] *Judgment? The Pretender to this world's throne will be judged.*

Here Jesus is described noting that the world resents his message, but reminding his disciples they won't face similar disapproval alone. He'll send them the Spirit of peace—the same Spirit that moves Jesus to do and say the things the disciples have witnessed. The Spirit will help them give a similar witness in their words and deeds. And they will need the Spirit's comfort because people will try to silence their witness by excommunicating them from the community of their fellow Jews, and will threaten them with execution [v.2]. Jesus tells them why their attackers will be so opposed to their message: they haven't come to know God as their Father, and won't listen to the Son rejoicing in the Father's promises [vv.3–4].

Readers who remember that, near the beginning of the supper, Peter asked Jesus where he was going (13:36) might wonder why the author of this section (Chapters 15 through 17) quotes Jesus saying that no one asks where he's going [v.5]. This inconsistency could entice us to analyze the intentions of this author. But an analysis of the text at this moment will distract a reader whose primary aim is to hear its Good News. The simple question we've been asking is: what does the Gospel as we have it in its present form tell us about the Good News? Here, the author spells out the Good News by describing Jesus assuring his disciples that he knows they don't want to confront the fact that he's going away [v.5]; and he knows they feel overwhelmed by sadness [v.6]. But he also knows they're not seeing his departure in the proper context. All the material in the first fourteen chapters of the Gospel portrays Jesus as a patient teacher. The author of this section doesn't alter that portrait. So, here again, Jesus quietly repeats his lessons. In this matter of accepting the news of his departure, Jesus asks the disciples to consider the paradox that his going away will not leave them alone. And he promises to send them the divine Spirit to comfort and enlighten them. He tells them how simple and practical this plan is: although they'll be working without him, this will be better for them. Why? When he goes and the Spirit comes, they will no longer have just his teaching, they'll have his own Spirit—the divine Spirit shared by the Father with him [v.7].

Perhaps the author felt that, no matter how often he repeated this astonishing promise of intimacy with God, it would continue to seem too good to be true—too unreal, especially in the face of the gruesomely real threats posed by the world. So he describes Jesus assuring the disciples they can leave it to the Spirit to prove God's case to the world beyond a reasonable doubt. It will be the Spirit, not they, who will make it clear to the world that lack of belief in Jesus is a sin; that it's right and just that Jesus should be raised to the Father; that doom awaits all who imagine they can rule the world [v.8].

All sin, of course, is the same: believing in oneself, not God [v.9]. The authorities have insisted they're right to say Jesus can't be united with the Father. Their "righteousness" will be revealed as wrong-headedness when Jesus is united with the Father [v.10]. As for judgment, the devil—or Satan, the lord of lies and the inspiration for all who love deceit—has already been convicted of falseness [v.11]. Jesus speaks of the spirit of evil the way a prosecutor speaks about a convicted criminal to a witness who fears retaliation: "Don't worry; the judge is going to put that one away for good."

JESUS ASSURES THE DISCIPLES THAT THEIR SORROW WILL TURN TO JOY [JN.16:12–24]

[12] *"I want you to learn many things," said Jesus. "But you're not ready to grapple with them now.* [13] *However, when the Spirit of Truth comes, that Spirit will take you through all truth. The Spirit doesn't make up the truth, but hears and speaks what the Father says, and then proclaims what will be.* [14] *[If you rejoice in me, you should rejoice in the Spirit, because] the Spirit will be glorifying me—taking all that I am, and imparting it to you.* [15] *[And what is 'all that I am'?] Everything the Father has is all mine—all that I am. The Spirit will take all that, and impart it to you.* [16] *So, in a while, you won't see me. Then, in a while, you will see me."* [17] *The disciples asked one another, "What's this, 'in a while you won't, but in a while you will'? And what's this, 'I'm going to the Father'?"* [18] *They kept asking,*

"What is this 'in a while'? We don't understand." [19] Jesus knew what they wanted to ask, so he addressed it. "You're asking one another why I said, 'In a while, you won't see me, and in another while you will.' [20] O, yes; O, yes. O yes, indeed, I'm telling you you'll weep and mourn even as the world rejoices. Your hearts will be pained. But your pain will turn to joy. [21] As a woman gives birth, she's in pain; her hour has come. But when the birthing is complete, the mother doesn't think about pain because of her joy—her baby's been born. [22] It's that way for you. Now [for a while] you feel hurt. But [in another while] I'll see you again and you'll feel joy—and that joy no one takes away from you. [23] When that day comes, you won't ask me a thing. O, yes; O, yes. O yes, indeed, I'm saying you'll ask the Father; and whatever you ask in my name, he'll give. [24] Up to now, [because I've been with you,] you haven't asked for anything in my name. Now, ask. You will receive. This is how your joy will be complete—like mine."

The author continues to present Jesus as eager to help the disciples imagine the difference between fleeting sorrows and lasting joy. Here Jesus makes an obvious point about the disciples' learning curve: they can't expect to learn everything at once [v.12]. They shouldn't fall into the trap in which the authorities seem tangled— that is, they shouldn't pretend they can know everything. Omniscience is a divine task and should be left to God. So, says Jesus, look forward to the Spirit continuing your lessons. The Spirit hears and speaks the divine truth—just as Jesus has spoken it. It should be a relief to the disciples to hear they're not expected to understand all truth—that they'll be able to continue learning about it, and learning from one who speaks only divine truth [v.13].

The disciples needn't fear they'll forget Jesus. Everything the Spirit will say to them will remind them of Jesus—will affirm and glorify all he said and did [v.14]. The Spirit will be imparting not mere information, but itself—the Spirit Jesus shares with the Father [v.15].

One might think Jesus could stop speaking at that point to let his disciples savor the extraordinary prospect of sharing God's own Spirit. And indeed the author seems to give Jesus words that suggest he's finished explaining why he can be leaving them but not abandoning them—why his departure will seem fleeting, since he's going to return [v.16]. But the disciples aren't ready to hear extraordinary promises. They can't figure out the logistics of Jesus' plan, so they complain to one another about his presentation of it. As far as they're concerned, Jesus hasn't been clear enough about the plan's timing, nor has he properly described its goal [vv.17–18]. The author's picture of their questions to one another is like a description of students protesting a difficult homework assignment. But Jesus—once again patient with his disciples' slowness to understand—tries the lesson another way.

He says he sees their confusion: they're distressed because they feel it's impossible to comprehend what he's saying [v.19]. Then he puts his message very simply. First, they will know misery while others have a laugh. But their misery won't be the end of the story [v.20]. He offers a familiar example of present sorrow leading to future delight: birthing. When it's time for a mother to give birth, there's nothing she can do to avoid the hour—it's time for bearing down. But there is something she can do. She can tell herself she'll soon see her baby. And if the agony of birth obscures the joy that lies ahead, it's nonetheless there. And soon she feels that joy—quite real, and crying for all her attention [v.21]. So, says Jesus to the disciples, "You do the same as that mother. Let the hurt happen. And, at the same time, let the thought of seeing me again and sharing my joy make you happy" [v.22].

Then Jesus asks them to imagine one more thing. They should think what it might be like to turn to the Father (just as he has) and ask the Father (just as he has) for what they want [v.23]. Ask, says Jesus, and see what it's like to be filled with my joy [v.24].

JESUS SAYS THE DISCIPLES STILL HAVE MUCH TO LEARN
[JN.16:25–33]

[25] *[After offering the image of childbirth and the vision of turning to the Father, Jesus concluded by saying:] "I've been using images to teach you. The hour is*

coming when I will stop using images—when I talk to you plainly about the Father. ²⁶ *When that day dawns, you will be asking in my name—and I don't mean I'll ask the Father for you.* ²⁷ *The Father loves you because you've loved me. You've believed I came from God.* ²⁸ *I come from the Father and into the world. I leave the world to go to the Father."* ²⁹ *The disciples said, "Now that you use no images, we do see plainly.* ³⁰ *Now we see you know all, even before someone asks a question. This makes us believe you do come from God."* ³¹ *"Now you believe?" said Jesus.* ³² *"Look," he said, "the hour comes—it's already here—when each of you will run off home. You'll abandon me. But I'm not abandoned. The Father is with me.* ³³ *[Don't fret.] I've spoken this way so that you'll find peace in me. In the world, you'll find trouble. But be cheerful. I've conquered the world."*

———

The author uses just a few sentences for Jesus to sum up what he's been saying to his disciples since they first gathered for supper. First, Jesus says the time for teaching with stories and examples is coming to an end. He's told the disciples over and over that he intends to send the divine Spirit, who will not need stories to breathe the truth into their very souls, to bring them a clearer understanding of the Father [v.25]. Then he says they'll experience this understanding as an impulse to rush directly into the Father's presence to ask him for his gifts of divine light and life [v.26]. And what they'll find when they run to their Father is a loving reception—a Father who says, "I know you! You believed in my Son!" [v.27]. In conclusion, he reminds them of his example: He came into the world because that's what the Father wanted; and now he returns to the Father because the Father wants that too [v.28]. Because they too are from the Father, they should rejoice that they're also going to him.

The disciples seem to understand this simple description of how a child of God behaves: if you're God's child, you recognize that you come from God, and you naturally go to God. This is no more complicated than saying a lamb bleats for the ewe that bore it. And the author says the disciples claimed to see the point plainly [v.29].

But, with one remark, the author reminds us how many declarations of "seeing" or "believing" we've read so far, and how many times Jesus mistrusted them. (Recall the crowd after Jesus removed the merchants from the Temple [2:23–25]; the well-fed crowd after Jesus prayed to the Father [6:14–15]; and the crowd at the Feast of Tabernacles [8:31–33].) Jesus has often asked people to rethink their assumptions about faith. Here, the disciples seem to believe Jesus because they think he can guess a question before it's asked: they say they believe because Jesus knows all "even before anyone asks him the question" [v.30]. Like so many before them, the disciples are still distracted by what they think of as Jesus' wonder-working powers. Although Jesus has told them repeatedly that he's doing the Father's works, not his own, they've apparently not yet understood this.

So Jesus returns to his task as a teacher. He gives them homework. Ask yourselves later on, he says, after you've abandoned me, "How strong was our belief in him?" [v.32a]. What a thing to hear! But Jesus isn't scolding his friends for not being true friends. To the end of his lessons with them, Jesus remains a patient teacher who cares for his students even when they are astonishingly slow. He doesn't want them to be upset when, in the near future, they realize how little they love him. Instead, he wants them to remember that learning to trust is the antidote to their lack of love. And they will learn to trust if they follow his example: he trusts the Father completely [v.32b]. He wants them to share this trust because it will bring them the same peace it brings to him. Trusting won't be easy, he says, because the world around them won't look peaceful. But, fear not! (Does this sound familiar to them by now?) He and the truth he's taught them about the Father will subdue this word's tumult [v.33].

SEVENTEEN

Jesus Once More Looks to the Father

JESUS LOOKS TO THE FATHER FOR GLORY [JN.17:1–5]

¹ When Jesus finished speaking to the disciples, he lifted his eyes to heaven and said, "Father, the hour has come. Glorify your Son, so your Son may glorify you. ² You've given your Son power over all flesh. [Why?] To give everyone in his care eternal life. ³ This is eternal life: knowing you, the one, true God, and knowing the one you sent, Jesus, the Christ. ⁴ I glorified only you on earth. I've finished this work you gave me to do. ⁵ Now, glorify me, Father—with your glory, the glory I shared with you before the world was."

———෴———

Earlier in the Gospel, John described Jesus turning to the Father in order to feed the hungry crowd (6:11). And he described him at the tomb of Lazarus turning to the Father as an example to the onlookers (11:41). Here, the author of this section of the Gospel describes the same thing: Jesus turns to the Father [v.1a]. Jesus' willingness to be utterly dependent on the Father is what reveals God's power and glory. Jesus has been described as doing nothing without the Father; he has insisted that all his words and works are from the Father. Each moment of his life—every hour—has been a moment with the Father. What's special about the "hour" that Jesus now faces is that his words and works will be violently ended, and still God's glory will be revealed. Despite the ugliness of the hour, it can't overcome the power of God. As John told us in the introduction, God's light "shines in the darkness." So Jesus lets God's glory shine—even though that means allowing himself to be condemned unjustly to death.

Those who fear death will instinctively feel that Jesus' attitude of trust is uniquely his, and impossible to share. Just above, Jesus himself was described saying that his disciples would flee from this moment (see 16:32). Jesus will have to die for us—showing us exactly how trust in God's glory works. Afterward, however, we'll realize he was right: neither death nor the way of the world can destroy him. Instead, he will have "conquered the world" (see 16:33). This is his hour; this is the reason he came to us: to reveal that the children of God will not only share their Father's glory after their lives, deaths, and resurrection, but can share in it now. Jesus' sharing of God's divine glory will be seen in this: his willingness to receive that glory just as God has chosen to give it—through a life, death, rising, and ascending in complete union with God. So Jesus asks the Father to continue his plan to reveal the divine glory in him [v.1b].

Jesus then thanks God for giving him the task of revealing that fleshly life is to be transformed into eternal life [v.2]. Eternal life, for which all flesh is created, is a life of knowing the Father and the Son intimately. The way we will know this relationship between the Father and the Son is not from learning mere facts about the relationship. We'll actually experience their relationship just as they do [v.3].

The depiction of Jesus praying in thanksgiving for having accomplished what his Father wanted him to do suggests that Jesus has nothing more to do. In a sense, his work is over [v.4]. Now that Jesus has proclaimed God's truth—the truth that God intends to fulfill his promise to give divine life and glory to his children—it's time for the Father to fulfill that promise. It's time for him to bring Jesus to glory through death and resurrection—to the glory God has always been sharing [v.5]. Jesus has been consistently portrayed in this Gospel as going about his work—the Father's work—energetically. But his day-to-day work of teaching his reluctant students is finished. His traveling is over. The conversation he's enjoyed with his disciples and friends can end now at any moment without a worry that something may have been left unsaid. As he faces the prospect of arrest and execution, Jesus needn't wrack his brain to discover where he went wrong with the authorities, or how he might have more persuasively led his fellow Jews to question their assumptions about scripture. As the author of this section depicts him here, Jesus isn't distracted by thoughts of what should or might have been. His prayer is an example of how we might pray—peacefully asking for trust and savoring the request with repetitions of it.

JESUS PRAYS FOR HIS DISCIPLES [JN.17:6–19]

[6] *Jesus continued to pray, "I revealed your name to those you gave me from this world because they were yours—you gave them to me. And they kept your word. [7] They're learning that whatever you gave me is, indeed, from you. [8] That's because I spoke to them only the words you spoke to me. They received them. And they're certain I came from you—that you sent me. [9] I pray to you for them. It's not the world I pray for. I pray for them—the ones you gave me, the ones who are yours. [10] Of course, all that's mine is yours—and what's yours is mine. This is my glory: you. [11] I'm not in the world now. But, as I come to you, they're still in the world. Father, Holy One, keep them under your name—the name you gave me—so they may be one, just as we are. [12] While I was with them, I kept them under your name—the name you gave me. I kept watch. No one was lost but the lost one; and, once more, scripture is seen to be true [i.e., some children of God choose to become children of lies; see Is.57:4]. [13] Now, I come to you. I say this here, in the world, that my entire joy may be theirs. [14] Because I gave them your word the world hated them, because they're not of this world any more than I am. [15] I'm not asking you to take them out of this world, only that you keep them from the Evil One. [16] They're no more of this world than I. [17] Bless them, set them aside, and make them holy with truth. Your word is truth. [18] I send them into the world just as you sent me. [19] It's for them that I dedicate and*

give myself wholly to the truth—yes, that they may be wholly consecrated to the truth."

———*◦◦◦*———

Here, the author describes Jesus praying aloud for his disciples, beginning with a statement Jesus has often repeated: he's been teaching only about God's glory; proclaiming who God is; revealing his name [v.6a]. And, says Jesus, not only have the disciples absorbed this proclamation [v.6b], they will continue to learn that his words are God's own words—that it is God who bends out of heaven to speak to them [v.7]. Jesus says to the Father, "Just as you are always speaking your word to me (see 1:1), I've been speaking to them. And they've accepted our word; they believe I speak with and for you" [v.8].

He prays for them, says Jesus, in a way that he doesn't pray for the world. He explains why he does this when he says again that they kept his word—they chose to believe. So when Jesus prays for them (showing them, by example, how they should pray for themselves), he reminds them that they should say to their God and Father: "I am yours" [v.9]. Then, lest we forget how complete and intimate is the communion between Father and Son, the author describes Jesus noting that when he says to the Father "mine," he means "yours"—and vice versa. In other words, there's no separating God's glory into parts. All of God's glory is Jesus' glory. This is the glory Jesus has wanted to share with the disciples—a glory the disciples are learning to accept [v.10].

Then the author describes Jesus praying as though he were already gone from this world [v.11a]. This can be interpreted to mean that his work in this world is over. But, in another sense, it's clear that he was never in the world—that is, the world of unbelief, self-satisfaction, and sin. Recall John's lament in the introduction that the world didn't recognize God's Word (1:10); his comment after the scene with Nicodemus that the world preferred darkness to light (3:19); his description of Jesus' warning at the Feast of Tabernacles that the world is addicted to sin (8:23); and Jesus' announcement soon after he was welcomed with palms into Jerusalem that the world was about to be judged and its ruler driven out (12:31). Note too that the author of this added section of Chapters 15 through 17 described Jesus alerting the disciples to this world's hatred of the truth (15:18–25). However a reader imagines Jesus' separation from the world, the fact is that he's leaving it. It's for that reason that Jesus believes his disciples will need divine aid—the protection of God's own name—to counter the world's illusions. Just as Jesus imagined helpless sheep needing the care of a devoted shepherd (10:1–18), he pictures his disciples needing divine care to keep them in accord with what he's proclaimed to them [v.11b]. He helped them to be one with each other—and with him—while he was with them. Now the Father must take over. True, one was lost. But you can't save or comfort someone who refuses comfort and safety [v.12].

As the author narrates it, Jesus' prayer is both personal and public; he's praying to the Father, but his disciples are listening. He prays in order that they may understand that praying is all about joy [v.13]. This is similar to the lesson Jesus tried to teach when he prayed aloud at Lazarus's tomb so that the crowd might learn what it was to trust (see 11:41–42). And the disciples will need the blissful comfort that comes from trusting because the world hates words that demand trust—whether those words come from Jesus or the disciples [v.14].

So, says Jesus to the Father, let them enjoy life in this world, but help them resist the lie that life in this world is all there is. Lead them from the embrace of deceit [v.15]. Because the disciples can't be satisfied by the stuff of this world any more than Jesus could [v.16], they'll need to be reminded that they're created for something more: divine truth, life, and glory [v.17].

At this point, Jesus is described feeling confident the disciples can head off into the world just as he did—to speak God's word and do God's works [v.18]. And why shouldn't he be confident? He says he'll dedicate himself—give himself—to the disciples as they face the mission he's just shared with them. Or, put another way, the Word of God—the divine Son who is always enjoying and expressing the power, life, and Spirit of the Father—will now give that power, life, and Spirit to the disciples. Incredible as that sounds, it also must be true. How could the disciples be wholly consecrated to divine truth unless that truth was theirs completely—unless they, like Jesus, were sharing divine life?

JESUS PRAYS FOR ALL WHO WILL BELIEVE [JN.17:20–26]

[20] [Jesus continued to pray to the Father.] "I don't turn to you and pray just for my disciples. I pray also for those who will hear their word and believe in me. [21] [I asked you to keep my disciples united in your name (see 17:11).] Now I ask you to unite all who believe. Yes, Father, just as you are in me and I am in you, united, one, together, let all believers also be in us, united, one, together. Let the world see this union and believe you sent me. [22] I've already given the disciples the glory you gave me. This is so they may be one, as we are one. [23] [Yes, one!] Myself in them; yourself in me. Let them be made fully one with us. Then the world will know that you sent me, and that you loved them as you loved me. [24] Father, I want those you gave me to be with me—to see the glory you gave me, yes, the glory you gave me because you loved me, even before you created the world. [25] Father, Truthful One, the world hasn't known you. I know you. And these, my disciples, are learning that you sent me. [26] And [because they've been willing to learn,] I've been able to make your name known to them. I'll keep teaching them about you. [But they won't merely be taking in my lessons.] They'll be taking in me—yes, the whole 'me' that is filled with you and your love."

Above (vv.6–19), the author described Jesus making a distinction between his disciples and "the world"—the world that has refused to believe. If readers missed that distinction, they can see it clearly here, as Jesus prays for all in this world who *will* believe because of what the disciples will later teach [v.20]. The author describes Jesus' prayer offering believers an example of how to pray. Following that example, believers would say, "Father, we believe you are with us—in us. Keep us always in your presence; keep us one with you.

Send us to bring your presence to others, just as you sent Jesus to us" [v.21].

Here Jesus prays as though he has already shared the Father's glory with his disciples [v.22a]. Readers who ask, "When did he do that?" should recall that, throughout this Gospel, we've been asked to notice how God's glory is already in the world—to notice how intensely God works to give his glory to his children. The introduction told us we see God's glory in Jesus (1:14); Jesus reminded Martha of his promise to reveal God's glory (11:40); and Jesus assured his disciples that they'd do the same work he's done—work that is divine and glorious (14:12–14). Divine glory isn't something we get as a reward. It's the state we're in when we're united with God—when we believe in him and let him fill us with the divine gifts he wants to give us.

As we picture the disciples hearing Jesus pray this part of his prayer to the Father, we can imagine them recalling that, when God gives gifts, he gives himself—all he is. That would include divine glory. Although the disciples can't fathom this truth, we're told they do believe it. According to Jesus, their belief makes them one with God—united with God just as Jesus is united [v.22b]. This relationship can't be explained the way a bond between two atoms or an alliance between two countries can be precisely drafted. No personal relationship can be so defined. Such a relationship is known only through experience of it. A good love story, or lyric, or poem can evoke some of the unique qualities of giving and receiving love. But nothing can tell the whole story of a relationship. Jesus isn't just telling the disciples about the relationship of love he shares with the Father. He's inviting them into it. And when the world sees them accepting that invitation, the world will know that Jesus is truly sent from God [v.23].

The author makes it easy for us to imagine that the disciples delighted in hearing this prayer. As Jesus comes to his conclusion, his variations on the theme of divine love, union, and glory build with the power of a musical finale. And all that power is directed at the disciples: "Let them be with me," says Jesus. "Let them experience our glory just as we do" [v.24]. The Father knows what's right.

The world, unfortunately, tries to make things right for itself—never turning to God for the truth. But Jesus does know God—and turns to him. He's also comforted that the disciples have accepted him as one who comes from God to share this knowledge [v.25]. Jesus still has much to share, and the disciples have much to learn. But their lessons will hardly be onerous because they won't be learning mere facts. They'll be realizing more and more clearly how passionately God loves them [v.26].

EIGHTEEN

Jesus Is Arrested, Abandoned by His Friends, and Brought to Trial

ARREST [JN.18:1–14]

¹ After Jesus finished speaking to his disciples and praying to his Father, he went out of the city with them, crossed the Kidron Valley, and entered a garden. ² Judas, his betrayer, also knew this place. Jesus went there often with his disciples. ³ Into that garden Judas guided a contingent of Roman soldiers plus Temple guards from the chief priests and Pharisees with lanterns, torches, and weapons. ⁴ Jesus knew all that was to happen, so he went up and asked, "Who do you seek?" ⁵ "Jesus of Nazareth," they said. "I am he," said Jesus. Judas, the betrayer, was still there with them. ⁶ When Jesus said, "I am he," they stepped back, stumbling. ⁷ So he asked them again, "Who do you seek?" "Jesus of Nazareth," they said. ⁸ "I told you I am he," said Jesus. "If you're looking for me, let these others go." ⁹ Jesus was honoring what he'd said [when, for instance, he was describing the Good Shepherd; see 10:28]: "I lose none of those you give me." ¹⁰ Simon, called Peter, had a sword. He drew it, slashed at the high priest's slave, and cut his ear. Malchus was the slave's name. ¹¹ Jesus told Peter, "Put the sword back in its scabbard. Shouldn't I drink the cup my Father gives me?" ¹² Then the Roman contingent and their commanding officer, plus the Temple guards, took Jesus and bound him. ¹³ First, they brought him to Annas, father-in-law of Caiaphas, that year's high priest. ¹⁴ Caiaphas was the one who warned the

149

Sanhedrin *[when the crowds were excited because Jesus had raised Lazarus from the dead] that one man should perish rather than the whole people of God [see 11:50].*

—————❧❧❧—————

In the previous section, we heard Jesus say this was his hour—the moment for him to accept death and rise to glory (see 17:1). Jesus has accepted his Father's will and made it his own. He's at peace. He doesn't need to do anything strange or extraordinary. So he does what he usually does in the evening when he's visiting Jerusalem— he settles in a garden with his friends [v.1]. Even though Judas knows Jesus' habits and routines, Jesus doesn't seem at all concerned about threats or danger [v.2].

Several times during the recent supper and its aftermath, Jesus was described making a distinction between the world of nonbelievers and his disciples. In this scene, John describes Jesus facing the world of unbelief as never before. Here, a large number of Roman soldiers has been sent along with guards from the Jewish authorities to arrest Jesus. John doesn't say how this force was put together, but it's obviously more imposing and has more authority behind it—both Roman and Jewish—than the rather ragtag group sent to arrest Jesus at the Feast of Tabernacles (see 7:32, 45–47). This group is fully equipped—even with plenty of lights [v.3]. Despite the numerical strength and official business of this force, Jesus isn't distracted from the business at hand—the business that's always at hand for him: the work of the Father. He confronts the arresting officers and soldiers with the same sort of direct question he asked his first disciples: "Who are you looking for?" [v.4].

John describes a formal recognition of who is who, then adds a detail that makes us realize there's no such thing as mere formal business between people. How eerie that, as the authorities play out a travesty of justice, Judas, the friend that helped to arrange this farce, stands by as though he were nothing more than a stage extra [v.5]. When "the world" plays with power and authority, it can be dangerous. Here, it looks ridiculous. It can't stand up to Jesus' simple declaration of the truth [v.6]. How peacefully and confidently he confronts the situation—both clarifying who he is and pointing out that, if it's him that's wanted, the disciples shouldn't be involved [vv.7–8]. He behaves just as he said a good shepherd should [v.9].

Perhaps John thought he needed to make clearer the distinction between the world's aggressive anxieties and divine peace. His description of Peter's gallant attempt to fight the world with the world's weapons is close to comic. Just as Peter's imagination failed him when Jesus wanted to wash his feet (13:8), here again he follows his own impulse rather than the example of Jesus. When John mentions another in the crowd by name, Malchus, he may be nudging us to notice that this encounter isn't a clash of anonymous forces and abstract principles. This is a family affair between individuals who know one another—some of whom profess belief in the same God and Father. Yet they've failed to see each other as God's children [v.10]. Jesus sets the example for anyone who wants to avoid a similar failure: set your eyes on what your Father desires to give you [v.11].

Then the powers of this world finally get their business done. There's an arrest [v.12]. People with political connections enter the scene [v.13]. Then John ends with a note that reminds us that sneaky scheming can accomplish its aims if you've got the power to back up your scheme [v.14].

PETER DENIES KNOWING JESUS [JN.18:15–19]

[15] *[After the arrest,] Simon (Peter) and another follower trailed after Jesus. Because the second follower was known to the high priest, he entered with the arresting troop—and Jesus—into the high priest's courtyard.* [16] *Peter, however, stayed outside the gate. The second follower (the one known to the high priest) went out, spoke to the woman at the door, and brought Peter in.* [17] *The door lady says to Peter: "Aren't you this one's disciple?" "No," says he.* [18] *Other slaves and servants were warming themselves around a fire built to fend off the cold. Peter joined them and warmed himself.* [19] *Meanwhile, the high priest questioned Jesus about his followers and his teachings.*

—=⟋⟍⟋⟍⟋=—

In this scene, John begins to describe life for the disciples without Jesus. The world must now be negotiated with the aid of powerful connections [v.15]. Things happen only because people can pull the proper strings [v.16]. However, influential contacts can't protect one from prying eyes and other people's curiosity. "I know you!" says the nosy gatekeeper. Peter doesn't seem to be in the mood to talk about either Jesus or himself, so he tells a lie [v.17]. It's the only sensible thing to do. This woman's question doesn't merely impose on Peter's privacy, it's a threat to his well-being. If he answered truthfully, he would have to confront the truth the way Jesus did, thus exposing himself to the same sort of misunderstanding and disapproval that Jesus faced. Better to pretend no connection to him.

So Peter does what anyone would do on a chilly night; he seeks warmth and comfort [v.18]. That's certainly a much more sensible choice than exposing oneself to the tedium of explaining what you believe and why you have felt the need to teach those beliefs [v.19].

JESUS' TRIAL BEGINS [JN.18:20–24]

[20] *[In response to the high priest's questions about his teaching and his disciples,] Jesus said, "I've spoken to the world publicly. I've taught in synagogues and in the Temple—wherever Jews come together. I said nothing secretly.* [21] *You don't have to take my word. Ask those who heard me speak. Certainly they'll know what I said."* [22] *A servant standing close by cuffed Jesus for speaking as he did. "You talk that way to the high priest?" said the man.* [23] *"If I spoke wrongly," said Jesus, "tell me what's wrong. But if I spoke rightly, why do you hit me?"* [24] *Annas then sent Jesus, still bound, to Caiaphas the high priest.*

—=⟋⟍⟋⟍⟋=—

John's mention of Caiaphas reminds us that this brief encounter with Annas wasn't part of the official investigation of Jesus. Annas retains the courtesy title of high priest because he once had that office, but he has no current official position. Nonetheless, John captures both the seriousness and the pretentiousness of this scene by repeating the title "high priest" six times in reference to Annas. The fixation on prestige and power in this circle of Jewish authorities is so intense that Jesus' suggestion that they ask others what he taught [vv.20–21] is considered an affront that merits a physical rebuke [v.22].

Of course there's no answer to Jesus' question about the reason for the violent reprimand [v.23]. It seems he simply has no right to ask a question or make a statement, no matter how sensible his inquiry or comment might be. This trial will not be a serious inquiry into what Jesus has said and done. It will be a diatribe against the things Jesus is accused of doing and saying.

Jesus' challenge to Annas is clear enough. He's asking him to ask himself what he truly wants. Is he fishing for facts—and, if so, which ones would he like to catch hold of? Or is he really interested? Like the newly seeing man turning the question back to the authorities, Jesus might ask Annas, "Do you also want to become a disciple?" (see 8:27). More importantly, that question is for us. Throughout this Gospel, John has been telling us about Jesus' public acts and words. Do we want to be his disciples? Annas wasn't interested in such a question, so he sent Jesus away [v.24].

PETER AGAIN DENIES KNOWING JESUS [JN.18:25–27]

[25] Peter was still warming himself by the courtyard fire. Some there said, "You're one of his disciples, aren't you?" "I am not," said Peter. [26] One of the high priest's servants was related to the servant whose ear Peter had cut. He says, "Didn't I see you in the garden with him?" [27] Peter again said, "No." Then, a cock crowed.

—✦✦✦—

Earlier, John described Jesus warning Peter not to overestimate his loyalty—to notice how easily he might lose interest in Jesus and become so obsessed with taking care of himself that he would repeatedly refuse to admit knowing Jesus (see 13:38). But this short scene isn't just the dramatic punchline to an earlier setup. Placed as it is, just after the brief, fruitless encounter of Jesus and Annas, Peter's lies, given in answer to direct questions, seem to be John's way of hammering home to us the ease with which we can miss, ignore, or flee the simple truth. Annas, and those around him, paid no attention to Jesus' suggestion that they ask others what they'd learned from his teaching. They were preoccupied with demanding the deference they assumed to be their due. Here, Peter can't speak the truth that would answer a straight question because he apparently fears for his safety.

We may find it easy to despise Annas for insisting that others defer to him. And we might easily sympathize with Peter, who only seems to want to avoid the possibility of getting dragged into a biased judicial proceeding. But the result in both cases is the same. Jesus' word is ignored. John has left us with a question: Is it sometimes sensible to brush Jesus aside—or is it never a good idea? How do you choose?

THE JEWISH AUTHORITIES BRING JESUS BEFORE PILATE
[JN.18:28–32]

28 At an early hour, Jesus was transferred once again. This time it was from Caiaphas's residence to the Roman governor's residence—the praetorium. However, the Jewish contingent didn't enter the governor's residence. That would have made them ritually unclean and kept them from celebrating the Passover feast. 29 Pilate came out of the residence and asked, "What's the charge against this man?" 30 "We wouldn't have brought him to you unless he'd been up to no good," was their answer. 31 "Then bring him to judgment under your own law," said Pilate. "We can't execute a death penalty," said the Jews. 32 Jesus' word about dying was thus borne out. [In 12:32, Jesus is described saying he would be "lifted up"—like the bronze serpent in the wilderness that proclaimed to God's children that healing and salvation were from their Father; see 3:14–15; Num.21:4–9. "Lifting up" would happen in the Roman execution of the death penalty—i.e., crucifixion.]

—⚬⚬⚬—

John skips whatever legal business might have unfolded at the official high priest's residence. This is the sort of omission that frustrates readers of fiction. "Wait!" we cry. "What exactly did Caiaphas say to Jesus?" But the evangelist isn't merely telling a good story. The only thing he wants to tell us is how Jesus proceeded to glory despite the machinations of others.

He tells us how punctilious the Jewish authorities were about observing the niceties of the Law. Although they seemed content to connive at getting an innocent man put to death, they were unwilling to violate a rule that forbade them to enter a Gentile residence [v.28]. So, noblesse oblige, Pilate caters to their delicate sensibilities, and comes out to them [v.29a]. He gets directly to business, asking why they're there [v.29b]. But the Jewish authorities have no taste for directness. They fudge their response by accusing Jesus of nothing more specific than being bad [v.30]. Pilate must push them to state their case [v.31a]. Only then will they admit what they want: a death sentence—and the governor's official approval of it [v.31b].

This exchange, like Jesus' encounter with Annas, and Peter's lies to the people around the fire, contrasts direct speech with prevarication. But then John reminds us that no amount of twisted scheming can alter God's plan to raise his children to glory. Because Jesus trusts in this plan—because he lets himself be completely caught up in it—he reveals the way to a full share in God's life, light, and glory. To those who put faith only in themselves, his lifting up will look like defeat. But it is a triumph of trust [v.32].

PILATE SPEAKS WITH JESUS, THEN SPEAKS WITH THE JEWS
[JN.18:33–40]

[33] Pilate went back inside the governor's residence, the praetorium. He called Jesus to him and asked, "Are you the King of the Jews?" [34] Jesus said, "Are you interested for yourself, or is this the report you've heard about me?" [35] "Am I a Jew?" asked Pilate. "Your high priest and your own people have brought you in to me. What did you do?" [36] Jesus said: "[You ask about kingship;] my kingdom

*isn't of this world. If it were, all who serve me would have fought to protect me from the Jewish authorities. But my kingdom isn't here." *[37]* "So, you are a king?" said Pilate. "You say 'king,'" said Jesus. "I was born and came into the world for this: to give witness to the truth. If you believe there is truth, you hear my voice." *[38]* "What's 'truth'?" asked Pilate. Then Pilate went outside to the Jews and addressed them: "I find no fault in him. *[39]* Now, you have a custom. At Passover I may release someone to you. Shall I release to you the King of the Jews?" *[40]* They yelled back, "Not this one. Give us Barabbas!" Barabbas was a bandit.*

We've read that the Jewish authorities dreaded a Roman response to Jesus' popularity and that they looked for a way to kill him (see 11:48–53). We've also read about the Pharisees' reaction to the crowd's acclamation of Jesus as "King of Israel" (see 12:13, 19). And we know that Roman soldiers were part of the group that arrested Jesus. We're not surprised, therefore, when John tells us that Pilate knows about this case. And Pilate gets directly to business: he asks Jesus about kingship [v.33].

Jesus' response is just as direct. John says Jesus wanted to know whether Pilate was truly interested in him or was merely doing his official duty [v.34]. This candid give-and-take continues with Pilate's honest answer: he's not personally interested in Jewish affairs. For him, this is purely a governmental matter of keeping good order. He only wants to know what Jesus has done to upset that order [v.35]. Jesus' answer to this direct question is a subtle but clear invitation to Pilate to rethink his idea of the proper order of things. From Pilate's point of view, worldly order is preserved by controlling others—a view Jesus would share if he too were interested in worldly power. But that's not the power he seeks [v.36].

Pilate isn't drawn into a consideration of other sorts of power. But he does want to know if Jesus is the sort of rabble rouser he's been accused of being. Does he accept the designation "king" [v.37a]? John then describes Jesus giving the same explanation of a true Jewish king that he tried to convey by entering Jerusalem on a donkey (see 12:15). A leader of God's people doesn't lead armies to battle. He leads his people to divine truth [v.37b]. Pilate has been described as interested in the facts of this case, but here he curtly dismisses any broader conversation. He avoids a discussion of truth [v.38a]. So he goes back to his job. First, he gives his evaluation of the facts: "Not guilty" [v.38b]. Then he plays the politician and tries to give the authorities a face-saving offer: declare Jesus "pardoned" rather than "innocent" [v.39].

Readers know what Pilate does not: the Jewish authorities have come to the governor not because Jesus was truly a threat to Rome, but because he challenged the Jews' authority (see, e.g., 7:30–32; 8:48–59; 9:39–41). The only deal they want from Pilate is the sentence of death they already asked for [v.31]. I suspect the evangelist was aware of the cold blast of irony here. God made a deal—a Covenant—with his people. The Covenant was this: they will be his people, and he will be their God. They need no other deals (see Dt.5:6–10). Here, God's people make a new deal for themselves: a freed bandit for the Son of God. Even Pilate, whose only interest is to keep the peace, seems to suspect that's not a good deal.

NINETEEN

Jesus Is Tortured, Executed, and Buried

PILATE TRIES TO MOLLIFY THE CROWD WITH TORTURE
[JN.19:1–8]

¹ Pilate had Jesus scourged. ² Soldiers wove a crown of thorns, put it on his head, and threw a purple cloak on him. ³ They filed up to him saying, "Hail, King of the Jews." And they kept punching him. ⁴ Then Pilate went out and said, "I'm bringing him out. I want you to know I find no grounds for proceeding." ⁵ Jesus came forth, wearing the thorny crown and the purple cloak. Pilate said, "Look at the man." ⁶ When the chief priests and the Temple guards saw him, they yelled, "Crucify! Crucify!" Pilate said, "Take him and crucify him yourselves. I find no evidence against him." ⁷ The Jews said, "We have a law. According to that law, he should die. He made himself out to be the Son of God." ⁸ When Pilate heard that, he became fearful.

—◦◦◦—

John describes Pilate going about the tricky business of handling an enraged group of influential people and the seemingly innocent suspect who had enraged them. Perhaps in the hopes of proving that Jesus was hiding no crime, Pilate had him tortured [v.1]. Although the soldiers are portrayed as brutes, they're merely doing their job of knocking sense into a potential troublemaker. They make a fool of Jesus, and they have a laugh at the absurdity of calling him a king [vv.2–3]. Pilate completes his ploy of degrading Jesus in order to show there's no evidence of wrongdoing by presenting him as a bloodied innocent [vv.4–5]. However, where Pilate sees innocence, the authorities see a sin worthy of death [v.6a]. Pilate is described making one more attempt to get this crowd to see the unreasonableness of their choice. He says, in effect, "I find him innocent. If you know better, proceed on your own" [v.6b].

Then, at last, the authorities make a precise charge: this man pretends to be divine [v.7]. As Roman governor, Pilate has an impossible task. First, he must respect the local religion. Second, he must keep religious fervor from flaring out of control—especially at large feasts such as Passover. And last, he has to keep up the pretense that the emperor is the only sovereign who is divinely chosen. Pilate begins to be anxious [v.8].

PILATE ABANDONS CONTROL OF THE JUDICIAL PROCEEDING [JN.19:9–16]

⁹ *Pilate went back into the governor's residence—the praetorium. He asked Jesus, "Where are you from?" But Jesus didn't answer.* ¹⁰ *"You won't answer me?" says Pilate. "Don't you see I have the power to let you go or to crucify you?"* ¹¹ *"You have no power over me," said Jesus. "All your abilities come from above. The great sin was handing me over to you."* ¹² *At this point, Pilate was looking for a way to release him. But the crowd of Jewish officials and guards were howling, "If you free this one, you're no friend of Caesar. Whoever claims to be a king defies Caesar!"* ¹³ *When Pilate heard that, he brought Jesus out. He sat on the judge's bench set up in the courtyard called "the Pave Stones," known in Hebrew as Gabbatha [or, the High Place].* ¹⁴ *The day was the preparation day for Passover. The hour was about the sixth [noon]. Pilate said to the Jews, "Look at your king."* ¹⁵ *They yelled, "Go on, go on: crucify him!" Pilate said, "Crucify your king?" The chief priests said, "We have no king besides Caesar."* ¹⁶ *So he turned him over to be crucified. They led Jesus away.*

—◦/◦/◦—

Pilate's first question here might be read as a stalling tactic, or as an attempt to learn more about Jesus' claim to be the Son of God. Or readers may sense that both impulses are at work. What's certain, however, is that John's portrayal of Pilate is changing. Pilate seems less straightforward and methodical as he begins to fish for facts [v.9]. When Jesus is silent, Pilate's businesslike detachment collapses as he tries to muscle his way to information [v.10]. With Jesus' response, John reminds us, first, that true power comes from God [v.11a] and, second, that the great sin, the only sin, is to turn away from God's power and put trust in yourself—as Judas did [v.11b].

At this point, Pilate seems lost. All he knows is raw, human power. He doesn't recognize the power of truth even when Jesus mentions it to him (cp. 18:37–38). So he bows to a power he can recognize—the menace of a mob [v.12]. He clings to the trappings of power—his bench on a raised platform [v.13]. But this is playing at justice. Pilate's not in charge; the mob is. Even the formal mention of the date and time highlights the fact that this human judicial procedure is in stark contrast to the divine action about to be celebrated at Passover [v.14].

Then, with one more turn of the screw, John increases the awful tension between divine and human desires [v.15]. He concludes the scene on what seems to be a note of complete victory for raw human power [v.16].

JESUS IS CRUCIFIED [JN.19:17–27]

[17] *Jesus had to carry a cross to a place called Skull (in Hebrew, Golgatha).* [18] *They put him on the cross with two others on either side—Jesus in the middle.* [19] *Pilate placed a placard on the cross. It said: "Jesus of Nazareth. King of the Jews."* [20] *Jews from all over [who were visiting Jerusalem for the feast] could see the sign because Skull, where Jesus was crucified, was just outside the city, and the placard was in Hebrew, Latin, and Greek.* [21] *The chief priests argued with Pilate: "Don't say, 'King of the Jews.' Write: 'He claimed to be King of Jews.'"*

²² "I wrote what I meant to write," said Pilate. ²³ The crucifying contingent of four soldiers divided up his clothes. But his long shirt was seamless, one whole piece of woven cloth. ²⁴ So they agreed not to tear it, but to gamble. "Let's throw dice to decide the owner," they said. This is the sort of behavior scripture describes when it says: "They share my clothes among themselves. They gamble for my garments" [Ps.22:18]. That's how the soldiers behaved. ²⁵ Also standing there at Jesus' cross was his mother, his aunt, Mary (wife of Clopas), and Mary Magdalene. ²⁶ Jesus saw his mother there with the disciple he loved. Addressing his mother, he said, "Ma'am, look: your son." ²⁷ Then addressing the disciple, "Look: your mother." From that hour, the disciple took care of her.

John begins this section with some details of Jesus' apparent defeat: he's forced to carry his instrument of death to the place of public execution [v.17], and he's exhibited with other condemned criminals [v.18]. Then John describes the political jockeying over the wording of the death notice. Readers can savor the sad irony that Pilate unwittingly wrote the truth about kingship while the Jewish authorities deliberately denied it [vv.19–22]. That bit of petty haggling is followed by another: four soldiers gambling for their spoils [vv.23–24a]. Obscured by all this fuss is Jesus. His dying has become a mere detail in other people's business.

John reminds the reader what scripture says about suffering at the hands of others [v.24b]. Though cynics may believe that, in this life, the victor always gets the spoils, Psalm 22 expresses a different belief. The Psalm assumes that we will feel abandoned by God—a feeling attributed to Jesus in other Gospels (see Mk.15:34; Mt.27:46). For instance, you may be brought so low that others will take your clothes and share them out as you watch. That would be a good time, says the Psalm, to call on the Lord for rescue, salvation, and life (see Ps.22:19–21). You will need comfort; so ask for it. As if to remind us of the sort of comfort we seek most, John describes the presence of family and friends near the cross [v.25].

Did Jesus' friends and family encourage him—say, with the words of a Psalm—to trust in the Lord? We have no way of knowing. But John does tell us Jesus reacted to the presence of his mother and a beloved disciple by speaking to them. Mary's last appearance in this Gospel was at the Cana wedding, but readers will probably remember something of that occasion—Jesus' first "sign," or miracle. Throughout the Gospel, John has made a distinction between the world's lust for works of wonder and Jesus' desire to do the work of God—works, or signs, that affirm God's presence and action in the world. It's not a stretch to think that, at this moment, John hoped we would remember that Mary, like Jesus, trusted that God is always present, always at work. When Jesus asks the disciple to see Mary as his mother, he's asking him to cherish her example—the example of belief that first taught Jesus to trust. Jesus says, in effect, "My mother, who gave me my first lessons in reliance on God, is now your mother" [vv.26–27a]. With this simple image, John tells us again that the disciples will have to keep learning to choose to share God's glory—to keep imitating Jesus' choice (see 17:4–8).

John concludes by saying that, from that moment, the disciple included Mary in his household [v.27b]. If that statement isn't merely a throwaway detail—if it's not added as the sort of routine business that preoccupied the soldiers, the Jewish authorities, and Pilate—then it tells us something more. It suggests that, as Jesus completes the work the Father asked him to do, it's now time for the disciples to continue that work. One way for disciples to remember what that work is, is to recall how Jesus began it at Cana: as a response to his mother's reminder that God's glory can be revealed in our struggle with everyday worries and needs (see 2:5).

JESUS DIES [JN.19:28–37]

[28] *Jesus knew his work was done. So that others might understand that scripture had already spoken about this divine work, he said, "I'm thirsty." [This was another prayer using the Psalms to turn to God in suffering; see Ps.22; 16.]* [29] *Nearby was a jar full of sour wine. They wrapped a wine-soaked sponge around a hyssop stalk and put it to his lips.* [30] *After he took the wine, Jesus said,*

"It's done." Then he bowed his head and gave up the spirit. ³¹ Because it was preparation day [for a Sabbath], and because the Jewish authorities didn't want the bodies to linger during that Sabbath—a solemn feast day—they asked Pilate to let the legs be broken [to hasten death] and the corpses taken away. ³² So soldiers broke the legs of the first man, then of the other crucified with him. ³³ But when they got to Jesus and saw he'd already died, they didn't break his legs. ³⁴ One soldier thrust a spear into his side, letting out blood and water. ³⁵ By the way, this is the testimony of an eyewitness—truthful testimony—so you too can believe the truth. ³⁶ These things showed that scripture speaks the truth [when, for instance, it says]: "No bone will be broken" [in the Paschal Lamb; Ex.12:46]. ³⁷ There's also the scripture text [from Zechariah that imagines God's people repenting after wounding him with their disobedience] which says, "They'll look on the one they pierced" [Zech.12:10].

Throughout this Gospel, John has placed great emphasis on Jesus' desire and ability to do God's work—and only God's work. In every moment of life, God's children can and should turn to their Father who desires to continue in them the divine work of creation until it is gloriously fulfilled. So Jesus turns to the Father in his act of dying. First, he prays using Psalms [v.28]. Then he allows himself to be ministered to by his executioners [v.29], who shared their thirst-quenching sour wine with Jesus, but may have had no interest in Jesus' deeper thirst for doing God's work. Last, Jesus completes the work the Father gave him by placing his life where it belonged—in the hands of the Father [v.30].

In a previous scene, John said it was the preparation day for Passover (see 19:14). Here we're told it was the preparation day for a Sabbath [v.31a]. The question "Which is it?" is beside the point. Jesus believed God's children were living in God's time. All moments of their lives were blessed by the God who makes all moments. Each year's feasts, every week's Sabbath, and each day's prayers were reminders that God was keeping a covenant with them—keeping a promise to care for them as his own. The point the evangelist is making is that both the Roman and Jewish authorities are preoccupied with marshaling time to suit purposes they've set for themselves; neither group is focused on God's purposes. John gives us two examples of how some official types behave as though life was merely a series of business transactions. The Jewish authorities go about the business of keeping the Sabbath holy by speeding up the executions. Their concern is to make sure the corpses are removed before sundown [v.31b]. The soldiers attend to their business by following orders efficiently—so efficiently that they waste no effort breaking the bones of a dead man [vv.32–33].

Then John mentions a third bit of business that might seem out of the ordinary—a spear thrust to verify that Jesus is dead [v.34a]. Although that action can be seen as nothing more than a confirmation of death, a reader may see a similarity between it and a Temple sacrifice. When a Jewish priest sacrificed an animal, the release of the animal's life blood was a reminder that all life comes from God. Because God is always giving his own life to his children, his children need not cling to life. A Temple sacrifice affirmed belief in the gift of divine life by letting an earthly life go. Here, a Roman soldier collaborates in this sort of sacrifice by allowing Jesus' life to gush forth—a surprising flood of both blood and water [v.34b]. Jesus could give up life-sustaining water and life-pumping blood because he was always taking in the gift of divine life. He could empty himself because he was being filled.

These details seem to be John's way of stressing that certain truths were revealed through this death. First, the fact—or truth—of Jesus' death is paradoxically verified by a startling sign of life's abundance. But, in addition, this death reveals that God's plan for sharing his life unfolds despite—or even in—the seemingly careless grind of daily business. "Yes," says John, "I have this from an eyewitness who saw it all and believed. And I now hope that you too will believe" [v.35]. Adding to the eyewitness, John cites the testimony of scripture. For scripture tells us again and again that all things unfold under the guidance of God—to whom we should therefore turn, and turn again [vv.36–37].

JESUS IS BURIED [JN.19:38–42]

38 Joseph of Arimathea, a disciple of Jesus who followed him secretly for fear of the Jewish authorities, asked Pilate if he could take Jesus' body away. When Pilate agreed, Joseph came to get the body. 39 Nicodemus (who had visited Jesus at night [see 3:1]) also came, bringing a hundred pounds of a mixture of aloes and myrrh. 40 Together, they took Jesus' body and bound it in linen cloths with the spices—as is the custom for Jewish burials. 41 Near the place he was crucified was a garden where there was a tomb in which no one had been interred. 42 Because it was the preparation day, and the tomb was nearby, they put Jesus there.

———ᐁᐁᐁ———

Here John depicts more ordinary business. Everyday life goes on without much evidence of life's true, extraordinary nature. People are busy dealing with matters that press for attention.

Even if readers didn't know from the Gospels of Mark and Luke that Joseph of Arimathea was a Jewish official (see Mk.15:43; Lk.23:50), they might reasonably assume his official status in the Jewish community by his ability to speak with Pilate about the disposal of Jesus' body [v.38]. From Nicodemus's previous appearances in the story (see 3:1; 7:50), readers know that he too is an official [v.39]. As we read about their actions, we may not pay much attention to the fact that, in order to arrange matters as decently as these two Jewish officials wish, they have to use large amounts of money and political clout. These two men, with their obvious influence and apparent wealth, can manage the practical business of both removing Jesus' body in a timely fashion and locating a convenient burial place, yet still giving it the care that custom calls for [vv.40–42].

It takes the wiles of this world to hustle Jesus' lifeless body quietly out of the way.

TWENTY

The Tomb Is Empty; Jesus Appears to His Disciples

JESUS IS NOT IN THE TOMB [JN.20:1–10]

¹ Early on the first day of the week, Mary Magdalene came to the tomb. It was still dark. But she saw that the stone had been moved away from the tomb's entrance; ² so she ran to Simon Peter, and to the disciple of whom Jesus was most fond. She said, "They took the Lord from the tomb; we don't know where." ³ Peter and the other disciple went to the tomb. ⁴ The two ran, but the other disciple ran faster than Peter and got there first. ⁵ As he bent down, he saw the linen cloths lying there, but he didn't go in. ⁶ Peter came up after him and, going into the tomb, saw the linen cloths lying there. ⁷ But he also saw the head cloth lying apart from the other cloths, folded in its place. ⁸ Then the other disciple entered, though he'd arrived first. He saw, and he believed. ⁹ Up to that point, neither of them understood what the scriptures were telling them: that he had to rise from the dead. [Take, for instance, Psalm 16 proclaiming, "You won't abandon me to Sheol or let your servant see the pit," Ps.16:10; or the Book of Hosea saying, "On the third day he will raise us up," Hos.6:2.] ¹⁰ Then the disciples went back where they were staying.

⎯⎯⎯✶✶✶⎯⎯⎯

John describes one of the witnesses of Jesus' execution, Mary Magdalene, coming to the tomb, perhaps to mourn, at the earliest moment permitted by the Sabbath law. She's startled to find the tomb's stone has been removed [v.1], and, assuming someone has broken in, she goes for help [v.2]. Peter and the disciple whose special bond with Jesus we've been hearing about since the supper (see 13:23) rush to confirm the theft [v.3]. The disciple with Peter arrives first, but stops at the tomb's entrance and notices the burial cloths lying there.

This description of a disciple arriving first at the tomb but not entering it may tempt readers to interpret the scene symbolically. But we can't know what symbolic or theological meanings the evangelist found in the details he relates to us. However, we can see what's obvious: these two disciples are doing the best they can to understand what's happening. And that, I think, is the point: they're doing the best *they* can do. They run; one runs faster [v.4]. The faster disciple looks—but only looks—into the tomb and sees burial cloths [v.5]. Peter runs up to the tomb, goes into it, and sees the burial cloths, but also notices the head cloth, folded [vv.6–7]. The other disciple then enters the tomb, sees the whole scene, and believes—though we're not told what he believed [v.8]. These details are a step-by-step process of puzzling out a mystery. The two disciples work at what they do best—figuring things out for themselves.

In case we don't notice that these disciples haven't yet learned what Jesus tried to teach them—had not, for instance, taken to heart the comfort of which Jesus assured them during their most recent supper and conversation—John points it out to us. They still didn't understand scripture as Jesus had understood it: as a promise that the life we're living is in complete control of a God who loves us [v.9]. So the disciples go back to where they'd been—apparently unchanged [v.10]. True, John tells us the second disciple believed. But his belief wasn't a response to God's word [v.9] but to the evidence before his eyes. His belief at that moment seems to have been of the grudging sort—the sort that expresses itself as a bewildered admission: "Well, I guess there's no other explanation." That's different from Jesus' expressions of trust in the Father—say, for example, when he said, "Father, the hour has come. Glorify your son" [17:1]. That belief is not yet the disciples' belief.

MARY MAGDALENE SEES JESUS [JN.20:11–18]

[11] Mary stood outside the tomb, weeping. As she wept, she bent and looked in. [12] She saw two angels in white at either end of where the body had been. [13] They said, "Woman, why do you weep?" She said, "They took my Lord; I don't know where they put him." [14] Just after saying this she turned and saw Jesus, but didn't know him. [15] Jesus said, "Woman, why do you weep? Who are you looking for?" She thought it was the gardener. "Sir," she said, "if you took him, tell me where. I'll take him." [16] "Mary," said Jesus. Turning, Mary said, "Rabbouni," Hebrew for "Teacher." [17] Jesus said, "Stop holding on to me. I haven't yet ascended to the Father. Go tell my brothers, 'I go to my Father, and your Father; to my God, and your God.'" [18] Mary Magdalene told the disciples, "I've seen the Lord"; and she related what he said.

————

Like Peter and the other disciple, Mary Magdalene tries to make sense of events. Her inability to do so makes her weep [v.11]. Even after God's messengers nudge her to question her distress, she fails to do so. If only she knew where they put him, then she could stop being anxious [vv.12–13]. She's so distracted by her frustration, she doesn't recognize Jesus. Of course she doesn't recognize him. She's not truly seeking Jesus. Instead, she's trying to answer a problem for herself. But there is no problem. Jesus is being lifted up to the Father—to glory. Although Mary of Magdala is clearly a follower of Jesus, she, like the other disciples, is slow to learn what Jesus taught about trusting in God's plan. She's focused on her plan: to find Jesus' body and take care of it [vv.14–15].

Finally, the proper relationship between Jesus and a disciple is reestablished: Jesus calls her by name (just as the good shepherd calls his own) and she calls him Teacher [v.16]. But Mary has the impulse to grab at what seems right rather than to let God do what's right. Jesus has to tell her to let him go, just as he asked those at the supper to let him go (16:7). Mary must let go of the plans she's concocting in her head and accept God's plan to glorify his Son.

When John describes Jesus saying he hasn't yet ascended to the Father [v.17a], he's not saying Mary is delaying Jesus. What's captured succinctly in Jesus' words to Mary is the same sort of command to love that Jesus gave at the supper (see 13:33–34): "Despite your worries, you must let me go. Instead of worrying about yourself, love one another—tell one another I'm going to my Father, your Father" [v.17]. And that's what Mary did [v.18]. She told this Good News. What could be simpler?

JESUS APPEARS TO OTHER DISCIPLES [JN.20:19–31]

19 In the evening of that first day of the week, Jesus appeared in the midst of his disciples, though the doors were barred for fear of the Jewish authorities. He said, "Peace to you." 20 He showed them his hands and his side. They glowed with delight at seeing him. 21 "Peace to you," he said again. "As the Father sent me, I send you." 22 He breathed on them and said, "Receive the Holy Spirit. 23 Whose sins you let go, they're gone. If you hold on to them, they're held." 24 Thomas, one of the twelve, who was also called Didymus, "the Twin" [see 11:16], wasn't there when Jesus appeared. 25 So the other disciples told him, "We've seen the Lord." But he said, "Unless I see the mark of the nails in his hands and put my finger in there, and put my hand into his side, I'll never believe you." 26 Eight days later, the disciples were again together behind closed doors—Thomas with them. Jesus again stood in their midst and said, "Peace to you." 27 Then he said to Thomas, "Push your finger in and probe my hands. Put your hand into my side. Don't be unbelieving. Believe." 28 Thomas said, "My Lord; my God." 29 Jesus said, "Have you believed because you've seen? How blessed are those who don't see, but believe."

30 Jesus did many other signs during the time [before his death] that he was with his disciples—signs not described in this book. 31 But these were written that you might believe that Jesus is the "Christ"—God's "Anointed One"—the Son of God. Have life in his name by believing.

—◦◦◦—

These two appearances describe Jesus' last encounters with his disciples. (A description of yet another appearance was added later to the text. It's recounted in the material gathered in Chapter 21.) In these two scenes, John describes how Jesus equipped the disciples to overcome their fears and live their daily lives as disciples.

His first appearance is sudden, with Jesus responding immediately to the disciples' need for peace [v.19]—the gift he promised at supper (see 14:27). They are filled with divine peace and joy when he shows them his wounds—wounds that paradoxically confirm that, though he died, he is with them now, living [v.20]. Then he again gives them the gift of peace so that they can contentedly accept his commission, just as he accepted the Father's [v.21]. As he promised, they won't be alone on their mission. He asks them to receive the Holy Spirit [v.22], the Comforter he spoke of at the supper (14:16–17). Then he gives them a command that describes how life is lived in the peace of the Holy Spirit: they are to forgive sins [v.23a]. They can, of course, choose to hold on to sins. It's for them to choose [v.23b]. Notice that Jesus doesn't waste time with recriminations, corrections, or even advice. Though the disciples haven't given any evidence that they are ready for the task, he asks them to behave as he has behaved: "Go, do the reconciling work of the Father. You are filled with divine peace and the Holy Spirit. Go!"

His second appearance can be understood as a response to the continued confusion and anxiety of his disciples, especially as it's expressed so baldly by Thomas. John apparently wants us to recall precisely who Thomas is: "Surely you remember Didymus. He's the one who boasted he was ready to die with Jesus (see 11:16); the one who complained at the supper that Jesus wasn't being clear (see 14:5). He now demands proof of Jesus' Good News" [vv.24–25].

In this scene, John depicts the deep, abiding difficulty of believing the Good News; and he describes what believers should do about it. First, no matter how worried and distracted you are by the perils and burdens of this world, even if you feel you must lock yourself away from the world's threats, be at peace. Accept God's peace [v.26]. Then, if you're like Thomas—if you'd like proof that you can trust God to bring you peace—admit your need. Act it out. Say what Thomas said. Feel what it's like to stand up to God and make demands. Then, choose: be demanding, or believing. Jesus suggests believing [v.27].

Thomas, in a word, says yes to the invitation to believe [v.28]. Jesus says, "How blessed you are to believe—to say yes. And now, all of you who have not yet said it, say yes. Experience the blessedness of believing" [v.29].

John then concludes his work. He hopes that what he's related about Jesus' signs of working in God's name [v.30] will help us choose to believe that Jesus speaks for God, and that accepting and trusting in his word is accepting God's life [v.31]. John ends as he began (see 1:3–4). He makes the simple but breathtaking assertion that, when God communicates, he doesn't give information about himself. He gives himself.

TWENTY-ONE

A Variation on Jesus' Commission to His Disciples

DAILY BUSINESS AND DIVINE BUSINESS [JN.21:1–14]

¹ One time, [after the resurrection,] Jesus appeared to the disciples at the Sea of Tiberias. This is how it happened. ² Simon (Peter), Thomas (the "Twin"), Nathanael (from Cana in Galilee), the Sons (of Zebedee), and two other disciples were together. ³ Simon Peter said, "I'm going fishing." They said, "We're coming with you," and got on board. They caught nothing all night. ⁴ As dawn broke, Jesus stood on the shore. They didn't recognize him. ⁵ He said, "Hey, boys, caught any fish?" They said, "No." ⁶ He said, "Cast the net to starboard and you'll find fish." They cast the net, and suddenly there were more fish than they could haul on board. ⁷ The disciple Jesus loved said to Peter, "It's the Lord." When Peter heard it was the Lord, he grabbed his robe [he was working without it] and dived into the water. ⁸ The other disciples also headed in (they were only a hundred yards off), hauling the net behind them. ⁹ When they landed, they saw a charcoal fire with fish on it, and bread. ¹⁰ "Bring some of your fish," said Jesus. ¹¹ Simon Peter dragged the net on shore. It was full of fish: a hundred and fifty-three—but the abundance didn't break the net. ¹² Jesus said, "Come eat breakfast." None of the disciples attempted to ask, "Who are you?" They knew: it was the Lord! ¹³ Jesus took the bread, and gave it to them. He did the same with the fish. ¹⁴ This was the third time Jesus appeared to the disciples after being raised from the dead.

173

—◦◦◦—

Scholars don't know when the description of Jesus appearing to his disciples at the Sea of Tiberias in Galilee was added to the text. But even though we can't be certain when and how it was decided to include this episode, we can tell simply from reading the translated text why it might have been added: it repeats and affirms the message in the previous accounts of Jesus' appearances. We can imagine an editor saying, "Here's another example of the resurrected Jesus coming to his disciples [v.1] to strengthen their belief." (This appearance should be counted as the fourth if we include Jesus' appearance to Mary Magdalene, the first disciple given the mission to proclaim the Good News of Jesus' glorification.)

The manner of listing the disciples' names might call to mind a newspaper's list of notorious characters: Tony (the Boot), Willy (the Old Man), Frankie (the "Kid"), and so on. It's as if the author wanted to say, "You know these fellows. What do you think they did? That's right, they went fishing" [vv.2–3a]. But their fishing was fruitless; they had worked to no purpose [v.3b]. At this moment of disappointment, Jesus appeared [v.4a], but the disciples didn't recognize him [v.4b]. The author doesn't explain the lack of recognition. It may, however, remind us of Mary Magdalene's mistaking Jesus for the gardener—that is, no one is expecting to see Jesus.

The author describes Jesus asking a natural question, getting a simple answer [v.5], then making an ordinary suggestion that leads to an extraordinary result [v.6]. The beloved disciple suddenly realizes that Jesus is speaking to them. Perhaps Peter's reminded by the unexpected catch to expect the unexpected; then he rushes to grab the moment [v.7]. The other disciples come ashore with less frenzy. The author is telling us, perhaps, that practical business such as landing a boat and a net of fish needn't be abandoned in order to notice and savor Jesus' presence [v.8]. In fact, Jesus himself is portrayed happily engaged in a daily chore: fixing breakfast [v.9].

The author then suggests that divine business happens in the midst of ordinary business. Jesus says, "Let's use some of that huge catch you just made" [v.10]. We needn't explore the description of

Peter hauling in a big net for symbolic meanings. We can enjoy it for its ordinary surprises: Peter hauled the bulging net ashore (an unexpected display of strength); the net contained 153 large fish (a surprising amount in a hand-tossed net); and the net didn't tear (a reminder that it's difficult to explain why everyday events happen) [v.11].

The author describes the disciples accepting Jesus' invitation to the meal with a mix of bafflement and trust. It's as if they're thinking, "Jesus can't be with us. But he is with us" [v.12]. Jesus feeds them as he once fed the hungry crowd [v.13]. Perhaps they recalled what he did then—how he first turned to the Father and "gave thanks" (see 16:11). The author of this added scene has chosen details that call to mind what Jesus taught repeatedly: he is the source of divine life, nourishment, and glory because he has received and accepted these gifts from the Father. Believe in him, and share the gifts of glory, light, and life. The author implies that it was to strengthen this belief that the risen Lord appeared to his disciples several times [v.14].

JESUS GIVES A COMMISSION TO PETER, AND TO US
[JN.21:15–25]

 15 After they ate, Jesus said, "Simon, son of John, do you love me more than these?" He said, "Yes, Lord. You know I love you." "Feed my lambs," said Jesus. 16 A second time, Jesus said, "Simon, son of John, do you love me?" He said, "Yes, Lord. You know I love you." "Take care of my sheep," said the Lord. 17 A third time, Jesus said, "Simon, son of John, do you love me?" Peter was sad that he asked a third time, "Do you love me?" He said, "Lord, you know all. You know I love you." "Feed my sheep," said Jesus. 18 "O, yes; O, yes. O yes, indeed, when you're young, you put on clothes and strut where fancy takes you. But when you're old, you need help. Someone else takes care of you, and you go where you're taken." 19 He was describing how even his death would give glory to God. Jesus then said, "Follow me." 20 Peter happened to notice the beloved disciple— that is, the one who was next to Jesus at the supper and asked about the betrayer, "Lord, who is it?" 21 Peter asked, "Lord, what about him?" 22 Jesus

said, *"Even if I want him to be here when I come back, how does that matter to you? I've said to you, 'Follow me.'" ²³ This answer started a rumor among the believers that the disciple who Peter asked about wouldn't die. Of course, Jesus didn't say he wouldn't die. He said, "Suppose I wanted him to wait until I returned." ²⁴ By the way, this is the disciple whose testimony is the basis of these writings—and his testimony is true. ²⁵ Jesus did many other things that, if written down, one by one, would overwhelm the world.*

The author's description of Jesus repeating his question to Peter gives the exchange a formal, almost ritual character [vv.15–17]. But the repetition of the questions and answers doesn't seem intended merely as a solemn reconciliation after Peter's triple denial of Jesus (see 13:38). We can certainly imagine Peter's feelings of shame and chagrin. But the author only glances at them with a reference to sadness [v.17a]. What the author emphasizes by the repetition of Jesus' command is that, if Peter loves him, he should take care of his flock. Without directly alluding to Peter's failure to love, the author here contrasts it with Jesus' triumph of forgiveness. Jesus' triple question-and-command, while revealing his awareness of Peter's tepid love, also reveals his desire for him to learn true love. This is the love Jesus described at the supper, when he spoke of laying down his life (see 15:13). If Peter wants to love, he will have to act as Jesus did—he must care for others. And when it comes to following the command to forgive (see 20:23), what better example to follow than Jesus' own example here—letting go of Peter's sin, not holding on to it.

What sort of life will Peter be choosing if he accepts the commission to become, like Jesus, a good shepherd? The author tells us how Jesus described that life as it might unfold for any of us. At first we live as though life is all about us—our clothes, our travels, and so on [v.18a]. But that life gets turned on its head, and others make our choices for us [v.18b]. Finally, the inexorable arc of life takes us to death [v.19a]. The author then comments that this whole trajectory gives glory to the God who created this life. If Peter wishes to share in God's glory just as Jesus does, he should accept life just as God created it. Or, as Jesus puts it simply, "Follow me" [v.19b].

The author portrays Peter as still a bit slow to accept the simplicity of the divine plan. He'd like to know what's in store for the beloved disciple [vv.20–21]. So Jesus, still the patient teacher, restates his lesson about not being anxious to discover the particulars of God's plan for giving us his life. Jesus asks Peter to consider a theoretical question: "If you found out it was God's plan to let this other man live until I returned—as I promised to do (see 14:3)—what would that possibly have to do with you? Follow my example. Let God work in you. Yes, follow me" [v.22].

According to the author of this chapter, many people tried, like Peter, to interpret the divine plan by reading a hidden meaning into Jesus' words about not trying to read God's mind [v.23]. Then the author writes, "Dear reader, please don't think that I have tried to read God's mind. I'm reporting only the eyewitness account of the disciple I've just mentioned [v.24]. Of course, no one could possibly capture all Jesus said and did" [v.25].

Index

About the Author

Paul J. McCarren, SJ, works at Loyola Retreat House and at St. Ignatius Church, both in Maryland, while continuing to write Simple Guides to the Bible. A Jesuit priest, he has spent many years in both parish and campus ministry.